THE STARTUP COACH

Carl Reader

THE STARTUP COACH

Carl Reader

Teach Yourself®

DEDICATION

This book is dedicated to my long-suffering family – my beautiful fiancée Sarah, who has been an amazing support through the writing of this book, and my wonderful children (Jordan, Lauren, Daisy and Charlie), who are the reason why I do what I do every day. I'd also like to dedicate this book to my wider circle of friends and family, who have provided me with support and inspiration along the way, and my clients and colleagues over the past years, from whom I've learned so much, and I sincerely hope that they have also benefited in some way. Thank you everyone.

First published in Great Britain in 2015 by Hodder and Stoughton. An Hachette UK company.

First published in US in 2015 by The McGraw-Hill Companies, Inc.

Copyright © Carl Reader 2015

The right of Carl Reader to be identified as the Author of the Work has been asserted by him in accordance with the Copyright, Designs and Patents Act 1988.

Database right Hodder & Stoughton (makers)

The *Teach Yourself* name is a registered trademark of Hachette UK.

British Library Cataloguing in Publication Data: a catalogue record for this title is available from the British Library.

Library of Congress Catalog Card Number: on file.

1

The publisher has used its best endeavours to ensure that any website addresses referred to in this book are correct and active at the time of going to press. However, the publisher and the author have no responsibility for the websites and can make no guarantee that a site will remain live or that the content will remain relevant, decent or appropriate.

The publisher has made every effort to mark as such all words which it believes to be trademarks. The publisher should also like to make it clear that the presence of a word in the book, whether marked or unmarked, in no way affects its legal status as a trademark.

Every reasonable effort has been made by the publisher to trace the copyright holders of material in this book. Any errors or omissions should be notified in writing to the publisher, who will endeavour to rectify the situation for any reprints and future editions.

Typeset by Cenveo® Publisher Services.

Printed and bound in Great Britain by CPI Group (UK) Ltd., Croydon, CR0 4YY.

John Murray Learning policy is to use papers that are natural, renewable and recyclable products and made from wood grown in sustainable forests. The logging and manufacturing processes are expected to conform to the environmental regulations of the country of origin.

Hodder & Stoughton Ltd
338 Euston Road
London NW1 3BH
www.hodder.co.uk

CONTENTS

MEET THE COACH

My life in business started very early, in a very humble way. I can't lie and pretend that I was a child genius, but I guess the entrepreneurial spirit has always been with me. I grew up on a council estate in Shoeburyness, Essex, and as kids we would buy bottles of Happy Shopper lemonade to split into glasses, so that we could sell them to the other kids who weren't allowed to the shops on their own. Later, at the age of about ten, I had moved to an area called Rayleigh, where I would go around the neighbourhood with friends washing cars to earn money to buy magazines and sweets. I guess that with these experiences, I learned a lot about finding a market, the benefits of a captive market, providing a product, pricing strategies (we had already cottoned on to different levels of washing, and differential pricing for different sized cars!) and keeping customers happy.

I was never particularly academic, despite always doing reasonably well in exams and tests, and left school early to start a YTS (Youth Training Scheme) in hairdressing, returning simply to complete my GCSE exams. After applying for every job in the local paper, I had an interview at two accountancy practices and the Army (I must have worked in alphabetical order!). I was clearly more suited to advisory work as I was offered both accountancy jobs, and from there I started looking after businesses of all shapes and sizes.

I'm now fortunate enough to be a joint owner of a large local practice, which in 2013 won an award for Independent Firm of the Year (South West) in the British Accountancy Awards, in 2014 won the 2020 Most Innovative Medium Sized Firm award, and is truly the UK's market leader in its niche markets of children's tuition businesses and franchised businesses. Through this I've also been featured personally in Accountancy Age's '35 under 35', which is a showcase of young talent in the industry, and at the time of writing am a finalist for the British Accountancy Awards Practitioner of the Year, whilst the firm is up for the British Accountancy Awards Independent Firm of the Year 2014.

I've also been involved in other businesses, together with sitting on the board of two not-for-profit organizations, acting as a funding panel member for the Fredericks Foundation, and as a committee member for the British Franchise Association.

Carl Reader

ACKNOWLEDGEMENTS

I would like to firstly thank David Tovey, who inspired me to write a book of my own and proved to me that it can be done. During the planning stages I was helped by both Liz Gooster and Heather Townsend, who helped me understand more about the publishing industry and also the sheer amount of effort required to write a book!

During the preparation, I worked with a number of people who helped to clarify my thinking and provide an objective view on areas within their expertise, and for this I would particularly like to thank my business partner Ben Herbert and my marketing guru Chris Cook.

I would also like to thank my first two pre-order customers (that I know of), Nick Williams and Chris Lennon, who I am sure will enjoy both the book and the mention!

Finally, it wouldn't be a complete acknowledgements section without recognizing all of those who gave me moral support through the writing process, whether face to face, by telephone or on social media. So, it's left for me to thank all of those who gave me encouragement and the willpower to complete the book - it is truly more of a marathon than a sprint.

HOW TO USE THIS WORKBOOK

Congratulations on picking up this workbook! Within this book you will find a range of information and Coaching Sessions to help you take your idea from a concept through to a successful startup. Before diving head first into the content, it's important that you understand a little about how this book has come about, and how best to use it so that you can gain the maximum benefit from it.

I've advised thousands of businesses over the last 15 or so years, on a range of matters from simple bookkeeping and administration through to selling and even potential flotation on the stock markets. Over this time, I've seen the good, the bad and the ugly when it comes to business; and I'd like to share this information with you so that you can learn from the vast experience that I've gained along the way.

Whilst working with all of my clients' businesses, I notice some common trends amongst them, which prevent them from reaching their potential. Firstly, the entrepreneur often limits themselves through limiting beliefs. This might be due to a lack of goal-setting, not thinking outside of the box, or simply due to circumstances, whether past or present.

I also notice a strong tendency for the business owner to make themselves indispensable, by creating jobs and processes to avoid what is actually important in the early days – picking up the phone, speaking to prospects, and doing the work! Business is very simple when you step away from the details and remember that the goal is to attract and keep customers.

The book is structured as an interactive workbook, with Coaching Sessions for you to complete, interspersed with commentary. These are designed to be sometimes provocative, and have been set out in a way that will lead you to a sense of completion at the end of each chapter.

I would strongly recommend that you read the whole book in order, to ensure that all areas are covered, even if you feel that you have already satisfied a certain area.

Broadly, Chapters 1 and 2 are an evaluation of you and your idea, to make sure that it is appropriate to continue. These chapters will be reasonably provocative, forcing you to explore whether you are cut out to run a business, and whether the business idea is the right idea to be a success. Within these chapters we'll explore what your personal motivations are, whether you are in the right position to start a business, what sets your business apart, and whether there is space for it in the market.

Following this, Chapters 3 to 6 are preparation for your business, taking you from an idea that is feasible through to obtaining funding. We'll explore how you should structure your support team and how to perform market research. We'll also consider the business plan, looking at how this should be prepared and what should be included. Finally, we'll consider the various options that are open to you for sourcing funding for the business.

Chapters 7 to 10 are about action, and are deliberately structured in reverse order, as it is important that you can manage the business before you promote it. In these chapters, we'll cover the essentials of running a business. You'll learn the basics about managing your finances and your team. We'll also cover the systems that are needed to make a business a success, and the promotion of the business.

Finally, Chapters 11 and 12 consist of further reading, a review of activities undertaken within the book, and some reflection on how to keep sane once you are in business! This is where we tie the various chapters together and make sure that you continue in the right direction.

Please bear in mind that pretty much every chapter within the book could be a book in its own right, and there are plenty of further resources that you will be signposted towards at the end of each chapter, should you wish to explore a particular area further.

At the end of the book there is a list of further reading that I believe you will find useful in your journey as an entrepreneur, and I also have a website www.TYCoachbook.com/Startup which contains more content and advice for you to use in your business journey, together with some templates and other goodies.

Finally, it would be great to hear your success stories from using this book! Please feel free to contact me using the following methods. I'd love to hear from you.

Twitter: www.twitter.com/CarlReader

Facebook: www.facebook.com/CarlReader

Website: www.TYCoachbook.com/Startup

1 ARE YOU SUITABLE TO RUN A STARTUP?

✔ IN THIS CHAPTER YOU WILL LEARN

- Whether you are in the right position to start a business
- What motivates you to do what you do
- The difference between employment and self-employment

Before investing time and money into a new business, it is important to establish whether you are the right person to be in business. Despite the glamorous image that entrepreneurs such as Richard Branson and Lord Alan Sugar may have, the reality for many startups is that they struggle to survive. In fact, it is said that one in three new businesses fails within the first three years. It takes a certain type of character to ride the storm of being in business.

If you've been in employment for the last few years, ask yourself the following questions:

- Have you ever had other people actively competing against you for your wage packet, which might be less than National Minimum Wage?

- Have you ever had to rely on the phone to ring to earn money that day?

- Have you ever had a job pulled away from you with no notice whatsoever?

- Have you ever had an employer decide not to pay you for a month or two, leaving you to send begging letters until they do?

- Have you ever had to do absolutely everything for your employer, from cleaning the toilets to making the strategic plans?

The harsh reality of being in business is that customers are very different from employers. If an employer was to do some of the things listed above, the best that they could hope for is some negative press attention... but more likely, they might have an employment tribunal to attend. In business however, the above list is an example of the day-to-day issues that you could encounter.

It's not all doom and gloom though. Provided that you can handle the stresses of being in business, there are significant rewards for those who get it right. Most people who go into business would never go back to employment, and in fact many make themselves unemployable! The freedom that owning your own business gives you allows you to choose when you will work, who you will work for, and how you will work. You can potentially also earn far more money than you could in employment, with a saleable asset if the business is successful.

PERSONAL FINANCIAL REVIEW

The first step that any prospective business owner should take is to review his or her own personal position. This is also the information that the banks will need should you decide to approach them for funding.

! COACH'S TIP

Running a business is very different from employment. There is no comfort blanket, and you are ultimately responsible for your own destiny.

Therefore it is essential that you have an understanding of your personal position before going further. It is also vital that you consider others who may be reliant on you and your income.

COACHING SESSION 1

Personal review

Step 1

Prepare a list of your current monthly personal expenses, and your potential expenses if you were to trim back your lifestyle as far as possible. Be ruthless during this Coaching Session. If there is any expense that isn't essential, cut it out of the 'minimum' budget:

	Current Expense	Minimum Expense
Rent/mortgage		
Electricity/gas		
Telephone/internet		
Council tax		
Water rates		
Household insurance		

Life/critical illness insurance		
TV subscriptions/TV licence		
Petrol/diesel		
Car tax		
Car servicing and repairs		
Clothing		
Household goods		
Gifts (birthdays, Christmas, others)		
Food shopping		
Savings		
General spending		
Debt repayments		
Others (please list below)		
Total		

Does your other household income cover the expenses, or not? Any shortfall must be included as part of your working capital requirement when calculating your business finances (see Chapter 7), or must be covered through your 'net worth', calculated below.

Step 2

Now we have an understanding of your expenses, we need to look at your personal 'balance sheet'. List below what you own, and what you owe. It is important to be brutally honest, and realistic, when doing this as it is the only way of knowing what you have to fall back on.

What you own (assets)	Approx Asset Value £
1. Property (residential & investment)	
2. Savings	
3. Car	

4. Shares in listed / unlisted companies	
5. Other realisable assets:	
Total	

What you owe (liabilities)	Amount Outstanding £
6. Mortgage (residential)	
7. Mortgage (investment)	
8. Loans	
9. Credit cards	
10. Hire purchase agreements	
Other:	
Total	

Step 3

It's now time to get the calculator out. The following calculations will help you understand how much you can commit to the business:

a. Net Worth (Assets – Liabilities from Step 2)_____

This figure is your current 'net worth', which indicates whether you own more than you owe.

b. Bank review (the figure from part a. less any personal guarantees given) _____

This figure is the initial amount that the bank would consider that you are worth in any financial application.

c. Sensitized bank review (the figure from (b), adjusted to reduce any property value to 70% of it's total valuation _____

This figure is the amount that a bank would currently use (at the date of publication) as a reliable net worth, which they can depend on. This figure is often surprisingly low for most people, as the sensitizing of net worth affects property, which is usually the largest asset for many households. Don't worry if c. is negative, as there are ways of raising finance without security. You will however need to be aware that it could be more expensive. If (a) is negative, and you don't have sufficient income to meet your regular expenses, it would be worth reviewing your personal financial position more fully before proceeding with starting a business.

COACHING SESSION 2

Identifying stakeholders

Identify all potential 'stakeholders' of your personal finances (this may include dependent family members, creditors, beneficiaries of your will, amongst others), and consider whether you should consult them before starting your business.

Now that you have considered an up-to-date financial appraisal, it is time to think about the other aspects of self-employment. There are a wide variety of self-development books which focus on what makes us as humans tick. Generally, it is understood that a basic way of motivating people is to use the 'carrot' (i.e. something to aim towards) or the 'stick' (i.e. something painful to avoid). We'll start by exploring why you are looking to start a business.

COACHING SESSION 3

Personal ambition review

Step 1

What is the 'stick' that has made you decide to start your own business?

What will be the impact to you personally if you don't move away from this?

Step 2

What is the 'carrot' that particularly motivates you to start your own business?

What impact will it have on your lives, and the lives of those that you care about, if you were to make it happen?

PERSONALITY TYPES

If you've read any self-development books before, you'll know that there are a number of ways to classify different personality types. In his book *The E-Myth Revisited*, Michael E. Gerber identifies the following three types of personality:

- **Technician**. These are the people who enjoy doing the work. If they have a task to complete, they will do it well, and take pride in their work. They enjoy details, and getting to the bottom of difficult tasks. They are the ones who drive the trains.

- **Manager**. These are the people who thrive on order and systemization. They make sure that everything is in place for others to work as efficiently as possible. They can understand how different tasks and people can interact with each other. They are the ones who make sure that the trains arrive on time.

- **Entrepreneur**. These are the people who thrive on chaos! Unlike the other two personality types, they actively avoid details, and instead focus on idea creation and brainstorming. They challenge the status quo, and always look to find better ways of doing things. They are the ones who end up owning the train company.

When running a business, you need to know what kind of support you need in the early days. For example, if you are starting a lawn-care business, and you thoroughly enjoy lawn mowing, it would seem that your personality leans heavily towards that of a technician. A range of ideas and creative vision for the company might indicate an entrepreneurial slant. However, if you have had no managerial experience, and would rather not deal with staff and administration, then the managerial trait might be minimal. Therefore, a profile for such an individual could be 35 per cent entrepreneur, 10 per cent manager, 55 per cent technician.

🗩🗩 COACHING SESSION 4

What's your personality type?

How do you score? Allocate a percentage against each personality trait:

Technician_____%

Manager_____%

Entrepreneur_____%

There are no right or wrong answers for this, as everybody is different.

It is also important to have a grasp of this concept when you build your business. As you might have seen, the three personality types are very different. The technician could easily become upset with the manager's interference. The manager could become confused by the new ideas from the entrepreneur, which disrupt the system that has been developed. The entrepreneur could become frustrated with the overwhelming volume of details coming from the team. There are various permutations of this that can affect staff morale, and also help shape your future structure.

This is only one of a number of ways of profiling personalities. In Chapter 8 we will look at DISC profiling, which is another method of identifying how team members, including you, will get on with each other, and how they will approach situations.

WHAT IS THE DIFFERENCE BETWEEN EMPLOYMENT AND SELF-EMPLOYMENT?

Many prospective business owners are understandably cautious about starting their own enterprise, as it is a leap into the unknown. Traditionally, most children were brought up with the mindset of getting good grades, studying hard, and then finding a 'safe and secure' job. This upbringing naturally promotes being cautious of change and risk, and in turn may prevent you from starting your own business.

In his personal finance book *Rich Dad Poor Dad* (Warner Books, 2002), Robert Kiyosaki developed a model which he labelled the 'cashflow quadrant'. In this model he considers those income streams with one sole stream of income (employment and self-employment) to be on the left-hand side of the quadrant, whilst those with many streams of income (owning a business and becoming an investor) on the right-hand side of the quadrant. Kiyosaki's thinking is that whilst the traditional mindset is that a job or a self-employed professional role is 'safer', in fact it is the other side of the quadrant that is safer, as there is no chance of redundancy or other unforeseen circumstances which can cut off your sole source of income.

A question that might arise from the differentiation of self-employment versus owning a business is whether they are actually the same thing? Kiyosaki asserts that his definition of a self-employed individual is an individual who charges their time and efforts to a client, whereas a business owner has employees to perform the work required. This obviously conflicts with the common perception (and indeed sometimes the legal definition) of somebody being self-employed when they own a business, however for the sake of the cashflow quadrant model this differentiation is essential.

WHICH SHOULD I CHOOSE – OWNING A BUSINESS OR SELF-EMPLOYMENT?

You may already have an idea of what your aim is – whether it is to 'own a business' or to 'own a job'. There is no right or wrong answer in general, and some professions (such as the legal, medical or accounting professions) are usually a hybrid of self-employment and owning a business, due to the common requirement of the partners in the business to provide their own technical expertise.

An indication of what may be most suitable for you can be found from the results of Coaching Session 4. Some people believe that all self-employed people are entrepreneurs, however this couldn't be further from the truth! Michael Gerber, in *The E-Myth Revisited*, states that the E-Myth is actually the myth that all business owners are entrepreneurs. What you do need to consider though is that your personality type will indicate where your skill-set lies – if you are naturally inclined to enjoy technical work and detest managing people, it may be that becoming a self-employed professional is more suitable for you than employing a large team.

One of the best attributes of successful entrepreneurs is the ability to honestly appraise their own skills, and to be able to recruit others to perform roles that are outside of their talents or capabilities. Running a business requires far more skills than simply being proficient in the services provided by the business, or being knowledgeable about the product.

COACHING SESSION 5

What skills can I bring to the table?

Below is a list of some of the skills that I see as useful for entrepreneurs, in no particular order. Think carefully about the list below, and enter notes for those that you feel that you have experience in. Finally, tick the box in the final column for those that you feel need further development. We'll cover methods of development in more detail in Chapter 11.

Skill	Notes of experience	Development required?
Marketing and creativity		
Networking and relationship building		
Sales skills		

Office administration		
Staff management		
Change management		
Delegation		
Financial management		
Customer service		
Leadership		

OVERALL GOAL-SETTING

Regardless of the specific details of your business idea, it is important that you have an understanding of your own personal goals so that you know whether you are on track to achieve them. This process of goal-setting also allows you to understand whether or not your business goals are in alignment with your personal goals. Often, the cause of discontent in most entrepreneurs is due to a misalignment between their personal goals (which might be focused towards lifestyle objectives) and their business goals.

Therefore, I tend to look to explore personal goals and beliefs before discussing any details of the business – much to the surprise of most business owners, who want to shout from the rooftops about their business idea! By exploring these goals, and understanding more about somebody's personal motivations, it allows the business to be constructed in a way that will be in alignment with what they truly want as an individual.

There are many books available on goal-setting, and an author that specializes in this subject is Brian Tracy (see Further Reading at the end of this chapter). Space doesn't permit me to go into full detail about an effective goal-setting process here, however there are some key elements that deserve highlighting below:

SMART goals

For a goal to be effective, it needs to be focused, rather than just a general aim. The acronym SMART defines the attributes of goals that are ideally set:

S – Specific   A specific goal has a far greater chance of being achieved than a general target. Specific goals are usually more detailed than loose general goals, and will focus on the 'who, what, where, why and when' of a goal.

M – Measurable   A measurable goal allows you to know when you have achieved it, and perhaps more importantly allows you to determine whether you are on track with the achievement of the goal. For example, it is impossible to gauge whether you are on track to be 'financially independent' without a finite definition of the goal, or how much weight you must lose to be 'slim'.

A – Attainable   An attainable goal is a goal which will stretch you and challenge you, yet ultimately will be within your capabilities *at the point of completion*. This doesn't mean that you have to be limited to goals that you can achieve today, as we tend to grow and develop as humans so that we can achieve our future goals.

R – Relevant   A relevant goal is one that ties into your key objectives and beliefs in life. It must be a goal that you are motivated to achieve, and often this only comes about if it ties into your fundamental paradigms about how you should conduct yourself in day-to-day life.

T – Timely   Finally, any goal should be time bound. Without a limit to the time that a goal can take to acheive, the goal is left 'hanging' forever.

What timescales should I set for my goals?

One of the vital elements of setting effective goals is in relation to the timescales which you set for the fulfilment of the goals. I tend to personally focus on goals for one year, three years, five years and ten years; and it is fair to say that one of the downsides of my approach is that the long-term ten-year goals tend to be vaguer than the one-year goals, which are much more specific and adhere to the SMART principle.

> ## ! COACH'S TIP
>
> Something that I would stress from my own experiences is that you should always ensure that you don't run out of goals. I had a notebook of goals that I had set on holiday in my early twenties, and at the time the goals seemed very unrealistic. Having found the notebook aged 30, at the back of an old suitcase, I realized that I had an empty feeling because I'd actually achieved the SMART goals that were set within the notebook, but hadn't reviewed or replaced these. Therefore it is essential, as with business planning (as you'll see later in Chapter 5), to continually monitor and adjust your goals to avoid stagnation.

What sort of goals should I set?

Typically, when people first think of goal-setting they tend towards material items, or perhaps health related (giving up smoking, giving up alcohol, going on a diet etc.). I'd strongly suggest that you instead look at a more holistic approach, considering areas such as work–life balance, personal development, spiritual development, charitable aims.

> ## ! COACH'S TIP
>
> Always make sure that you only include goals that truly motivate you! Setting goals that look good on paper, but really only impress others, don't actually motivate you to achieve them. Instead, make sure that you are fully committed to achieving the goals that you set out.

Whilst your goals should always be SMART, I believe that you should always make sure that they are also challenging. The 'attainable' part of SMART is sometimes used as an excuse to set goals which don't challenge the individual. You need to make sure that you will be motivated and driven to achieve the goal, and its difficulty will in fact form part of that motivation (there are very few of us that can turn down a challenge!).

♀♂ COACHING SESSION 6

Goal-setting

It isn't within the remit of this book to undertake a full goal-setting exercise, however it is important that you plan and approach a goal-setting exercise properly. Below is an action plan – make sure you keep notes so that you can perform the Coaching Session properly.

1. First, you need to commit *at least* one full day to goal-setting, without distractions. Review your diary and set a date within the next month to do this.
2. Next, you should obtain a resource to guide you through this process. I've suggested a book by Brian Tracy (see Further Reading at the end of this chapter), however an online search will show a plethora of titles that can help you. There are also a number of free of charge online resources. Perform your research, and purchase/download the guide that you feel would suit you best.
3. Now that you have the guide and a day set aside for goal-setting, have an initial think about what your fundamental beliefs are, to prepare for this day. Spend some time thinking about what is important in your life, what items/people/activities you value, and what truly motivates you. There is no right or wrong answer, and no one will think any less of you if 'speedboat' is the answer!
4. Now that you have the date in the diary, set a second date one week later, which is your first accountability date. The most important part of any goal-setting process is the first step. Set a date when you will review your goals, and ensure that you have taken the first step towards their attainment.

→ NEXT STEPS

In this chapter you have pulled together a clearer picture of your own personal position before starting a business. The Coaching Sessions have allowed you to appraise both your financial position, and also your motivations for starting a business. By setting these out on paper, you can weigh up the pros and cons of moving forwards, because if you are not fully prepared for starting a business, it can have a devastating impact on your family life and your finances.

You have also been able to evaluate your experiences to date. You have probably seen that although a previous job may have focused on a specific role, the skills that are required by entrepreneurs are often used within these roles too. For example, a checkout assistant at a supermarket would be expected to provide customer service, financial accountability, relationship building and quite possibly sales skills!

This process of self-evaluation will allow you to identify any areas that you need to work on before proceeding with the business idea, before you get too far into this process.

We've also looked at goal-setting. I cannot stress enough how important it is to make sure that your personal goals are mapped out, and in Coaching Session 6 we set out a plan to get you underway with a goal-setting exercise.

Our next step is to evaluate the business itself, in much the same way that we have evaluated you personally as a business owner.

FURTHER READING

Directly referenced in text

Gerber, Michael E., *The E-Myth Revisited*, Harper Business, 2001

Kiyosaki, Robert, *Rich Dad, Poor Dad*, Plata Publishing, 2011

Kiyosaki, Robert, *Rich Dad, Poor Dad 2: The Cashflow Quadrant*, Plata Publishing, 2011

Useful resources

Personal development

Covey, Stephen R., *The 7 Habits of Highly Effective People* Simon & Schuster, 2011

Robbins, Antony, *Awaken the Giant Within*, Pocket Books, 2001

Canfield, Jack, *The Success Principles*, Element, 2005

Personal finances

Clason, George S., *The Richest Man in Babylon*, Signet, 2004

Goal-setting

Tracy, Brian, *Goals! How to get everything you want, faster than you ever thought possible* Berrett-Koehler, 2010

👍 TAKEAWAYS

What are my strong points as an entrepreneur?

What skills do I need to improve on?

What actions do I need to take going forwards?

2 IS YOUR BUSINESS IDEA FEASIBLE?

✔ IN THIS CHAPTER YOU WILL LEARN

- How to identify what makes your business idea different
- How to evaluate the business idea
- How to determine whether the business is scalable

In Chapter 1 we explored whether you are a suitable candidate for running a business. This is only part of the formula to success, as even the most successful entrepreneurs would struggle to run a poor business concept – let's be honest, no one can make a profit selling ten pound notes for a fiver! So, before we dive in to the finer detail of how the mechanics of the business would work, we need to make sure that the business idea actually works.

In my experience, the best businesses are often based on the simplest ideas. They do not have to be overly complicated or first to market to become market leaders:

- **Google** wasn't the first search engine – it was simply the easiest to use and best performing. Originally, it was in a very crowded market, with competitors such as Alta Vista, Lycos and Yahoo.

- **Amazon** didn't initially stock the widest range of products – however, it took the department store online as an extension of its original bookseller platform. Simply put, Amazon has put the High Street in everyone's home.

- **eBay** was a simple trading platform designed as a hobby to be the 'perfect market'. Its competition was traditional boot fairs, and in turn it developed to become a web store as well as an online auction house.

All of these businesses quoted above share a common theme. They are founded on a simple idea, which is unique and can be described to a child in a sentence or two. In the business world, these would be known as the 'unique selling proposition' and the 'elevator pitch'.

WHAT IS YOUR UNIQUE SELLING PROPOSITION?

Before you start your business, it is vital that you understand what makes your idea different from every other business out there. This doesn't necessarily mean that you come up with a completely new idea. Some businesses just do things ever so slightly better than others. It is often a small tweak on an existing, established model that can make all the difference.

Google is a perfect example of a business that is only *slightly* better than its competitors. When first released, it was amongst other search engines such as Lycos, Yahoo, AltaVista, Ask Jeeves and others. The difference was that Google had a unique interface, which was extremely simple to use, and it returned relevant results far quicker than any other interface.

The net result of this for Google was that they clearly positioned themselves as the dominant search engine, and in turn built a massive business that has significant influence over the internet, and indeed mobile telephones and tablets now. In fact, Google is often used as a verb instead of 'search' when people refer to finding some information online ... and, like Hoover, this is always a very good sign of a strong brand! The same can be said for eBay, as people will refer to 'eBaying' items rather than selling items online.

Establishing a unique selling proposition can sometimes take a lot of creativity and thought. For existing small businesses, it's not unheard of for the business owner to not actually know what makes them different from everyone else! To market your business effectively, and to communicate the value of your business and / or products to your customers, you do however need to be able to describe your unique selling proposition in a brief but clear manner, which is sometimes known as your 'elevator pitch'.

We will cover how to put together an elevator pitch later in the chapter, but first let's explore what makes your business different from its competition in the following coaching session.

COACHING SESSION 7

What makes your business different?

Some people instantly know what makes their business different. However, as demonstrated above, some very successful businesses are simply existing models with a twist or an improvement.

To get you thinking about how your business is different, consider the following questions:

What operational differences can you implement? Can you source exclusive distributorships, implement innovative systems, outsource labour costs effectively? Will you have new internal technology? How can you do things differently?

The above question will get you thinking about how your business can operate differently internally. It is essential to remember that this is only part of the equation, as customers do not tend to care too much about how you run your business. Instead, they want to know how you will benefit them as a buyer, when compared to your competition.

What different benefits do you offer your customer? Can you do it faster, cheaper, more conveniently? Can you utilize consumer-facing technology in a new way? What benefits will this give your end customer?

Of course, you need to make sure that the benefit is actually a genuine benefit compared to what is out there at the moment, and also that it is something that customers would value. There are several examples of products and services which either missed the mark, were marketed poorly, or were simply just before their time:

- **Atari Jaguar** – this was a 64-bit game console released in 1993. This might seem unremarkable at first glance; however at this time the market had only just moved to 16-bit consoles such as the Super Nintendo Entertainment System (SNES) and the Megadrive. It was a commercial failure, however by 1996 the Nintendo 64 was released, and soon after this was seen to be the minimum requirement for a 'modern' game console.

- **Amstrad E-mailer** – this was a device which allowed users to email from their landline telephone, via a pay as you go service – effectively a fax machine but for emails. It was a commercial failure, perhaps because its target market hadn't yet adopted emails, and would only do so when there was sufficient need and also when their intended recipients required it – by which time smart phones and tablets were commonplace.

- Finally one from my own industry (accountancy) – **IRIS iCash** – launched in 2002, this was an innovative product which allowed businesses to use an online accounting system to record their data. It was ahead of its time; however IRIS decided to pull the plug on this product circa 2008, and announced this with no replacement product in place. This lag period between announcement of stopping the service and introduction of new service coincided with the launch of several start-up services, using what is now known as the 'cloud', such as Xero and Kashflow.

! COACH'S TIP

Given that such successful companies can have commercial failures, it's evident that there is no such thing as a guaranteed business idea! You can however minimize your risk of a failure by ensuring that you do as much research and planning as you can before launch – remember: 'Failing to plan is planning to fail.'

WHAT IS YOUR ELEVATOR PITCH?

Once you have a clear idea of what your business is and how it is different, you then need to work out exactly how to communicate this to others. This is an essential skill at all stages of the business journey – from speaking to the bank manager for funding and persuading your partner, through the day-to-day running, and eventually when speaking to potential buyers of your business; you will need to be able to sum up exactly what you do and how you do it in a clear and concise manner.

An 'elevator pitch' is a brief statement which sums up your business in an easily understandable format. Although the concept of an elevator pitch is simple, creating one is often very difficult! To create a memorable pitch with impact, it is important that you focus on the benefits that your business can bring to its customers, whilst remaining clear about exactly what you do.

Examples of poor elevator pitches and how they could be improved are as follows:

- 'I am a gardener with 20 years of experience' could become 'I help people create low-maintenance gardens which the whole family can enjoy.'

- 'I am a local solicitor who specializes in contractual work' could become 'As an expert in contending legal contracts, I help businesses prepare watertight agreements based on my experience of pulling apart weak contracts – saving them time and money in the long run.'

- 'We are a marketing agency specializing in creative copy' could become 'By transforming the words that you use, we help you transform your sales letters from filling recycling bins to being top of your target's to-do list.'

Whilst this might appear obvious, it always surprises me how many businesses neglect their opportunity to make a great first impression at networking events with a strong elevator pitch.

COACHING SESSION 8

Create a strong elevator pitch

From Coaching Session 7, identify the one key benefit that your customer can immediately relate to:

Next, think about how to describe it succinctly, so that it has maximum impact. Perhaps relate it to either where they want to be (think time, family, money) or where they want to move away from (pain, hassle, debt):

Finally, try pulling it all together! This might take a few revisions until you feel comfortable with the final pitch:

WILL THE BUSINESS BE A SUCCESS?

Now that we've defined exactly what the business is and created an elevator pitch for it, we need to ensure that the business is actually viable before pressing ahead with it.

You are probably aware that setting up a new business is risky. Finding statistics to support this assertion is rather difficult, as many businesses either operate as unincorporated sole trades, or even under the radar in the black economy. However, a report from Business Zone, supported by the Department for Business Innovation and Skills (a government department), demonstrated that 20 per cent of new businesses fail within the first year, and 50 per cent of those remaining fail within three years. In order to avoid contributing to these failure statistics, there are three key steps that each new startup should follow:

- Consider whether the business is viable.
- Assemble a team of advisors (covered in Chapter 3).
- Perform market research to truly understand the market (covered in Chapter 4).

There are no guarantees of success when setting up a business – and sometimes the most carefully planned businesses are those that fail due to lack of action. As mentioned previously in this chapter there is an old adage that tends to be true for most businesses that I've seen: 'failing to plan is planning to fail'.

Although we'll look at market research in more detail in Chapter 4, it is important that you consider the basics of your market when preparing your initial appraisal of the business idea. It is almost certain that you would have some experience of the market, whether this has come from working within the industry, or indeed from being a customer of similar businesses. These first impressions of the competition can help shape your first thinking around the business.

COACHING SESSION 9

Competitor analysis

The first step in appraising your business is to take a look at your competitors. List your main competitors (big, small, online, offline – you need to consider each one):

What weaknesses do your competitors have at the moment? Are they trapped in an outdated model? Do they understand the local market needs?

What strengths do your competitors have? Do they have the benefit of a national brand? Are they well established?

What risks do your competitors pose to you? Is it possible that they can 'trade you out' (charging lower prices, or providing higher service levels, to stop you succeeding)?

Now you have thought about your competitors, it allows you to understand the wider picture of how your business will be placed. Together with Coaching Session 7, you would now be able to intelligently determine your own strengths and weaknesses. This will form part of your SWOT analysis (Strengths, Weaknesses, Opportunities and Threats) that we will complete later in the chapter.

The next step is to consider the external influences that can affect your business. These might not be immediate issues, as they could consist of impending changes, which can either be of benefit or detriment to you. Consider the following examples of external influences:

- Various businesses have repositioned to take advantage of the opportunities to reclaim unfair bank charges and payment protection insurance.

- A number of companies were formed to prepare Home Information Packs (HIPs) which were legally required to be provided as part of any home sale from 2007 – a decision that was then scrapped from 2010.

- Many businesses providing Garra Rufa 'fish pedicures' failed, after a major media report about the potential dangers of the treatment.

The SWOT analysis is a common feature of most business plans, and often a SWOT analysis is interpreted as an indicator of how well formed the thinking behind the business is.

The Coaching Sessions below are useful in understanding whether there is a market for your business, how it shapes up against its competitors, and whether there are any undue risks that might prevent you from moving forwards. What they do not cover is whether the business would be suitable for your ultimate goals, and whether it can meet your lifestyle and financial expectations.

When preparing a SWOT analysis, remember that the Strengths and Weaknesses are internal matters which relate to your business and are within your control, whereas the Opportunities and Threats are external matters. To help you analyse the threats of a business, you can perform a PEST analysis (see Coaching Session 10). A PEST analysis looks at political, economic, social and technological issues that might affect your business, and is a useful way of categorizing the various threats that a business might encounter.

COACHING SESSION 10

PEST analysis

1. Consider any **political** matters that could affect your business (e.g. regulation, deregulation, government intervention, tax policy):

2. Consider any **economic** matters that could affect your business (e.g. economic climate, globalization, staff costs):

3. Consider any **social** matters that could affect your business (e.g. demographic shifts, lifestyle choices, new trends):

4. Consider any **technological** matters that could affect your business (e.g. new consumer devices, technology trends):

COACHING SESSION 11

SWOT analysis

Using the answers from Coaching Sessions 7, 9 and 10, complete the following matrix of **Strengths, Weaknesses, Opportunities** and **Threats**:

Strengths	*Weaknesses*
Opportunities	*Threats*

IS THE BUSINESS SCALABLE?

One of the key weaknesses in a business with large goals is that the business itself may not be scalable. Before setting the vision and the goals for the business, an important part of the appraisal process is to determine whether in fact the business is scalable, and to what level the business can grow.

Often, a business is restricted by its limiting factors. These should have been identified within your SWOT analysis, however sometimes the business owner struggles to see these as clearly as an outsider can.

COACHING SESSION 12

Limiting factors

Below are some limiting factors that I typically see within businesses. You might well see some others once you put your mind to it and think about your own business idea. Tick the ones that you feel might be appropriate for your business at an early stage, and add any others at the end of the Coaching Session:

☐ Lack of capital

☐ Limited market size

☐ Limited available workforce

☐ Geographical limitations

☐ Technological limitations

☐ Management team/structure

☐ Business systems and processes

☐ Mindset limitations within the entrepreneur

☐ Lack of clear vision and focus

☐ _____

☐ _____

☐ _____

☐ _____

☐ _____

☐ _____

☐ _____

☐ _____

☐ _____

Now that you have identified the limiting factors within the business, it is possible to start working on how to resolve them. Not all factors, particularly external factors, can be resolved, however the first step is always to identify them, so that you can weigh up which factors can be resolved.

The potential scalability of your business will depend on the results of Coaching Session 12, and whether those factors can be overcome by you or not.

> **! COACH'S TIP**
>
> Typically, I tend to find that the main reasons that a business cannot scale are the entrepreneurs' mindset, the abilities of their management team, business processes and a lack of capital. We'll cover the scalability of businesses more in Chapter 9, when we look at systemizing processes within the business.

VISION AND MISSION STATEMENTS

Once you have considered your strengths, weaknesses, opportunities and threats, it is time to step back and contemplate the bigger picture. Your business doesn't *need* to have vision and mission statements – indeed, most of the planning in this book is optional – however, there is no way to measure the success of your business unless you know where you intended to get to. Also, if you plan to employ staff, persuade lenders, attract customers or motivate suppliers, you will need to get them to also buy into the vision that you have.

It is important to understand the difference between a vision and mission statement, which can be summarized as follows:

Vision statement

A vision statement is a future-looking statement, which summarizes the entrepreneur's 'preferred future'. It is often a lofty vision, and the entrepreneur needs to ensure that the mission statement of the business is in line with the overall vision, as the vision statement is simply the confirmation of the result of the business achieving its mission.

Mission statement

A mission statement is more current looking, and answers three key questions:

- What do we do?
- Who do we do it for?
- What is the benefit?

As you can see, the mission statement avoids any predictions about future success or aims, but instead focuses on what the business actually does on a day-to-day basis.

The best way to demonstrate the difference between a vision statement and a mission statement is to look at an example. In this case, I'll use an example of a (fictional) estate agency that is aiming to undercut their competition:

Mission statement preparation notes

What do we do? We act as agents for sellers, on a fixed fee basis. We don't attend viewings, nor do we have glossy brochures. What we do is act as facilitators between the buyer, the seller, and the solicitor. Our customers take their own photos and write their own descriptions, which is verified by us and optimized before being uploaded to our property portal. The whole sale process is managed by an online dashboard, which allows our sellers to monitor the process of their sale without picking up the phone to us.

Who do we do it for? Our target market is home owners with properties valued up to £250,000. Our typical customer is cost conscious, and happy to get actively involved in the sale process.

What is the benefit? Our customers receive a very cost-effective service, saving the average home owner £1,000 + VAT on their property sale. They also receive a unique tool which gives them visibility of the sale, whenever and wherever they wish.

Final mission statement

We are an online-only estate agency that charges fixed fees for property sales by using the internet to put home owners in control of their sale. Our average customer saves £1,000 + VAT, and has access to our virtual agency system at any time through their computer or smartphone.

Vision statement

Through our innovative technology and our aggressive pricing strategy, we aim to become the UK's leading estate agency by 2020, and will be the lead provider of estate agency software to other firms looking to provide a proactive service.

You can see from the above that the preparation required to write an effective mission and vision statement can be quite extensive in comparison to the final statement, which should ideally be a 30-second soundbite.

COACHING SESSION 13

Setting a vision and mission statement

Now it's time to start setting a mission statement and a vision statement for your business. Let's start with the mission statement, using the process detailed above. Bear in mind that you'd have covered a lot of this information through previous Coaching Sessions – the focus now is to express the statements in a clear and concise manner.

What do we do?

Who do we do it for?

What is the benefit?

Final mission statement

Vision statement

Now that you have clearly defined your vision and your mission statement, it's time to map out your goals for the business, and move on to the comparison of these targets against your personal goals and belief systems, as discussed at the end of Chapter 1.

We've already discussed the benefits of goal-setting, and in your business it is vital that you have ambitious goals to keep yourself moving forwards. It's also a great way of making sure that you are on track for achieving your overall vision. Using the online estate agency example, some business focused goals might be as follows:

Goals for year 1

To achieve 1,000 house sales for the year

To have a monthly average of 250 house sales for the final quarter

To operate on a monthly break-even basis by end of Quarter 3

Goals for year 3

To have built and launched a website to replace Rightmove, putting the seller in control

To achieve an average of 500 house sales per month throughout the year

To achieve an annual turnover of £6,000,000

Goals for year 5

To have a fully built prototype of the software system for other agents

To generate an annual profit of over £1 million

You can see from the above example that the goals become less specific in the longer time frames, and indeed if we were to set monthly goals they would become far more detailed. This is a common feature of goal-setting, and sometimes the long range goals need revising based on actual performance and market conditions – in this example, a possible revision could be that a competitor has already developed software for other agents. In this case, the company may decide to refocus and become a property portal for homeowners, effectively cutting out estate agents.

COACHING SESSION 14

Goal-setting for your business

Now that you have experience of goal-setting for your personal life, you should find that the process is simpler for your business. Map out some broad targets below for your business, based on different timescales (I suggest one-year, three-year and five-year). Make sure that the goals are SMART, and are sufficiently challenging to motivate you. Be sure to include goals that cover financial performance, work–life balance, and perhaps any prestigious activities that your business could be involved in:

Goals for year 1

Goals for year 3

Goals for year 5

◌◌ COACHING SESSION 15

Alignment of personal and business aims

Think back to the work that you performed in Coaching Session 6 of Chapter 1, and review the goals that you have just set for the business in Coaching Session 14. Are your business goals in line with your vision and mission statement from Coaching Session 13? Are your business goals in line with your personal goals? Have they taken account of limiting factors from Coaching Session 12? Is it possible to reach both your business and personal goals together, or do they conflict with each other? Write down any changes that you might need to make below:

→ NEXT STEPS

Having performed a personal review in Chapter 1, we have now focused on reviewing the business concept in this chapter. Much of this information will be expanded on in future chapters, notably during the sections on market research (Chapter 4), business planning (Chapter 5) and the scalability of the business (Chapter 9).

During this chapter we've also introduced the use of some basic business analysis models, such as SWOT Analysis and PEST Analysis. These are worth revisiting periodically, as the circumstances of any business change over time, as new opportunities and threats appear, and also as the business develops it can become stronger in certain areas and indeed lose focus in other areas.

Finally, we looked again at goal-setting, but this time from a business perspective. This Coaching Session should be taken as seriously as the goal-setting exercises in the previous chapter, and Coaching Session 6 of Chapter 1 provides a template of how to go about goal-setting should you need to refresh your memory on this. This groundwork will give you a good basis to prepare your business plan, which we cover in Chapter 5.

Next, we will be looking at how you can pull together an advisory team to help you establish and run the business.

FURTHER READING

Useful resources:

Business innovation and development

Godin, Seth, *Poke the Box*, The Domino Project, 2011

Priestley, Daniel, *Entrepreneur Revolution*, Capstone, 2013

Canfield, Jack, *The Success Principles*, Element, 2005

Paul, Debra et al., *Business Analysis* BCS, The Chartered Institute for IT, 2014

Goal-setting

Tracy, Brian, *Goals! How to get everything you want, faster than you ever thought possible* Berrett-Koehler, 2010

TAKEAWAYS

What are the weaknesses in my business idea that I can address?

Are there any threats that I need to be concerned about?

What actions do I need to take going forwards?

3 ASSEMBLING YOUR TEAM AND SETTING UP THE BUSINESS

✔ IN THIS CHAPTER YOU WILL LEARN

- Who should you bring into your team
- What questions to ask them
- Where to source free help – and when not to!

In the last two chapters we've established whether you are cut out to be an entrepreneur, and whether your idea has a chance of success. Providing that the answers to these questions are positive, it is now time to think about who you would like to bring into your team.

Often, when I suggest the notion of having a team to prospective new businesses, the owners recoil at first with the following objections:

- *I can't afford a team – I'm not even sure I can afford to survive yet!*
- *I'm doing this alone – nobody else understands my vision like I do!*
- *It's important that I do everything in the business, so that I understand how it all works.*

Whilst the above objections might seem perfectly reasonable, they are unfortunately indicative of a business that might encounter difficulties later.

! COACH'S TIP

I cannot recommend strongly enough the value of a team to support you, made up of professional advisors and other experts. Surprisingly, this will not cost as much as you might first perceive, and will ensure that you can learn along the way from people who have either been there and done it themselves, or from those who advise startups like yourself every day.

WHO SHOULD YOU BRING INTO YOUR TEAM?

The team should be broadly made up of two categories – professional advisors, and colleagues/business mentors.

The professional advisors that you will need to identify for your business would almost certainly include:

- accountant
- legal advisor
- banker.

It might be that the nature of your business requires another type of professional advisor – for example, someone to help you with compliance.

COACHING SESSION 16

Professional advisors

1. Write a list of the professional advisors required in your business, including those from the example above. Other areas may include HR, intellectual property protection, marketing, etc.

2. Now, identify the **business** requirements that you have of each. How would you like your advisory team to look? Traditional advisors? Modern approach? Large firm? Individual consultants? Industry specialists?

3. Finally, identify the **personal qualities** that you expect from your lead contact. Which do you value most in an advisor – bear in mind that no single advisor would normally have strong levels of all qualities, so which are important for you? Honesty? Politeness? Trustworthiness? Large personal network? Brevity? Experience? Optimism? Age?

By completing Coaching Session 16, you now have a stronger idea of what you are looking for in an advisory team, and this can help you narrow down your choices when you come to selecting them.

There are a number of ways of finding professional advisors for your business:

- **Word of mouth.** Being a professional advisor myself, this tends to be the most common route for new clients to find advisors throughout my industry. Speak to successful business owners that you know, and trust, for an honest opinion of their advisors, and if they are keen advocates of their advisory team, ask for a recommendation. If they are already in your industry, this recommendation is even more valuable for you.

- **Local networking groups.** Most towns have a variety of local networking groups that you can attend to meet business owners and professional advisors. This is a good way to meet the individuals before discussing business, but be wary of those who attempt to sell on the first meeting during the coffee break!

- **Industry networking groups.** It is very possible that your industry has a networking group within it, whether a trade association, or just a network set up by individuals within the industry. If you find an industry group, be sure to attend and find out a little more about the advisors who specialize in your field.

- **Online.** Generally, advisors who advertise on generic PPC (pay per click) key words via Google are aiming at a volume of clients, and might not give you the necessary service that you require as a startup. However, the online business community is strong, and by entering some of the business forums and social media sites, you will undoubtedly get to know some advisors through this route. Be conscious that any advisor can make their firm look bigger than it is online, in the same way some people project a perfect life on Facebook! So, be sure to do your research.

- **Professional associations.** Most professional associations or institutes have a list of members that is available either on their website or by post.

Use the above methods for each advisor noted in section 1 of Coaching Session 16, so that you can compile a shortlist for each team member. One thing it is important to avoid is being led by the cost of each provider's service. Although it is tempting in the early days to watch the pennies, it is unfortunately often the case that the cheapest advice ends up being the most expensive. This is not to say that all cost-effective services are not worth considering – I would instead urge you to consider what systems they have to allow them to offer the advice that you need over and above any compliance that they have to deal with.

Simply put, if one advisor values themselves at £15 per hour, compared to an industry average of say £200 per hour, you need to think very carefully about whether they are suitably experienced, and indeed confident enough, to deal with your affairs.

> ## ! COACH'S TIP
>
> It's worth mentioning a little about how professional advisors charge. Traditionally, accountants and solicitors have charged on an hourly basis. I'd strongly recommend that you push your advisors for fixed fee quotes, so that you know what you are committing to. Also, make sure that you have a mutual understanding of timescales, so that you can manage your expectations and know when to expect their work to be completed.

When it comes to sourcing a bank, most high street banks offer an initial period of free banking, of between 12 and 18 months. Some banks extend free business banking for life, yet others charge. The differences between the banks tend to be around service levels, and the amount of input you would expect from a manager. Banks also tend to tier their clients, with the smallest businesses being cared for by a call centre, whilst larger businesses might be one of only 20 clients for a manager. When selecting a bank, make sure that you find out exactly what you will be expected to pay, and the levels of service that you can expect from them.

WHAT QUESTIONS SHOULD YOU ASK PROSPECTIVE PROFESSIONAL ADVISORS?

To make your interviews with advisors as productive as possible, it is vital that you are prepared with a list of questions to ask them. This will help you gauge whether they are the right team member for your business, and also will help elicit responses which will enable you to identify whether they match the qualities that you have identified in Coaching Session 16.

Example background questions

- How long have you been working in this industry/region?
- Are you a member of your professional association?
- Have you worked with businesses of my type/size before?

Example questions about the organization

- How many staff members do you have?
- Will I be dealing with you or a colleague? If a colleague, can I meet them?
- What range of expertise do you have?
- Will your services still be a match for my business in two/five/ten years' time, as I grow?
- How will your firm deal with my affairs if you are away for any reason?

Example questions about start-up experience

- Can you tell me exactly how you help a typical startup?
- Can you provide me with a case study of a startup success?
- Do you have any services specifically designed for startups?

Example questions about your business

- How many businesses in my industry do you deal with?
- Are there any industry-specific issues that I need to be made aware of?
- Do you know the other advisors in my industry, and can you work with them?
- What issues do businesses similar to mine face?
- If you were in my shoes, what would you do?

Example commercial questions

- How do you charge for your services?
- What are your payment terms?
- When can I expect the work to be done?
- What happens if I'm unhappy with the service?
- Are there any potential conflicts of interests/do you work for any direct competitors of mine?

♋♋ COACHING SESSION 17

Asking the right questions

The above questions are a very generic starting point for your meetings with professional advisors. Consider any other questions specific to your business, and note them down here:

Asking the right questions *(cont.)*

WHAT OTHER BUSINESS ADVISORS SHOULD I HAVE?

Typically, when people think of business advisors, they think of the professions, and have an image of formal business advice. The most valuable advice however is from someone who has been there and done it themselves, as they can tell you their own story and what they would do differently. Perhaps most importantly, the advice that they will give you is often sincere and reflects the emotions behind various business issues, not just the logic.

Even today, I still have a strong 'advisory board'. This sounds much more impressive than it actually is, as in reality it is a group of friends in business who bounce ideas off of each other, and we always know that we can pick each other's brains.

Typically, the kind of expertise that you may need in a team, both in startup stage and as you grow, would be as follows:

- **Creator.** This is someone who can look at the big picture, carve out a vision for the future, and be decisive about issues rather than get bogged down by details (ideally, this would be the entrepreneur).

- **Marketing.** This person would be able to help you understand how to profile your target market, how best to reach them, and how to get the most out of your marketing spend. They will also encourage you to think about creative ways of marketing your business.

- **Culture.** This person would help you set a firm culture within the organization, and can also help you understand how to manage change as it inevitably arises during the growth of your business. They also are likely to understand the psychology behind the choices that employees, customers and suppliers make.

- **Process.** This person would help you critically appraise your business processes, identifying weaknesses and ensuring that there are clear lines of responsibility.

- **Finance.** This person would point you in the right direction should you need to raise funding, and also will be able to help you weigh up potential opportunities.

- **Technology.** This advisor would help you stay abreast of technological changes and can guide you with any issues that arise from your current operations.

These individuals can either be paid staff members, friends, or outsourced advisors. It might be that your own experiences allow you to fulfil one or more of these roles in your business as well.

COACHING SESSION 18

Creating an informal advisory board

Make a list of potential people, including yourself, who can fulfil the roles listed above, and highlight whether they would be staff members, informal helpers, or outsourced providers.

Creator

Marketing

Culture

Process

Finance

Technology

It's possible that Coaching Session 18 highlighted some areas in which you have no current contacts to fulfil the role. In that case, it would tend to suggest that this is either a new staff recruit, or more likely an outsourced service.

When selecting an outsourced service for these roles, the questions that you can ask the suppliers are identical to those for professional advisors.

BUSINESS ADVISORS, CONSULTANTS, COACHES AND MENTORS

If you do not have the right people for an informal advisory board, it would be worth considering paying somebody to provide guidance along the way. This however is a luxury in the early days of running a business, and any consultant or coach should be at least partly remunerated on a success basis.

Business advisors

Bank managers, accountants, and employees of government organizations typically undertake a business advisory role. They will help you through challenges that you may face in your business, based on their experience of dealing with many other businesses.

One of the problems of using these advisors is that often they have not actually run their own business, and as such revert to either theoretical answers, or simply share with you the experiences that they have seen their other clients go through.

Whilst this advice can sometimes be valuable, and indeed might come at lower apparent cost when compared to consultants and business coaches (indeed, it might be a 'free' service), you do need to consider that you are paying for the advice through your bank charges or accountancy fees, and also you need to weigh up whether the advisor is sufficiently experienced to assist you within your business.

Business consultants

Consultants tend to get a bad press within the media, as organizations such as the NHS use them to manage change processes within their teams. Often, these news reports will focus on the total cost, without looking at any benefit brought in from the consultancy team.

For smaller businesses, a consultant would typically be involved in either structuring the team of employees, or would assist in putting business process systems in place. A consultancy project is normally charged on a day rate, however some consultants will consider either a fixed rate for defined projects, or a success rate if the outcomes can be clearly measured.

Specialist consultants may also focus in areas such as finance, marketing, sales, technology, or operations. A consultancy project would ordinarily commence with a fact find, from which the consultant will prepare a report with the required actions.

Business coaches

Business coaches are a step on from business consultants, however I find that most business owners (and indeed some consultants/coaches!) aren't always clear on the difference between the two roles.

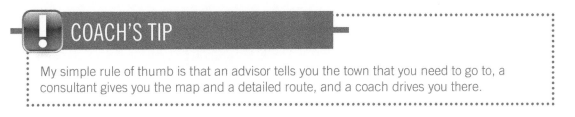

COACH'S TIP

My simple rule of thumb is that an advisor tells you the town that you need to go to, a consultant gives you the map and a detailed route, and a coach drives you there.

A business coach is focused more on the performance of the business and the leaders within the business. They will typically be engaged on an ongoing basis, and will be required to challenge and motivate the managerial team to develop both themselves and the business.

Mentors

The mentoring relationship is very different from advisory, consulting or coaching roles, as the role of the mentor is not to provide the answer, but simply to develop the mentee's understanding and clarity through effective questioning.

A number of voluntary mentors are available, and this is a role that is often fulfilled by experienced business professionals and entrepreneurs, as a way of giving back to the business community. I've personally been involved with the Frederick's Foundation, a national charity, and provided mentoring services to their startup businesses. Each area will have different mentors available, and this is an area that should be researched fully before committing to any paid advisors.

COACHING SESSION 19

Professional guidance

Do you feel that you need a consultant, coach or mentor within your business? Think about the role that you would need, if any, and make a note of the experience and type of person that you would like to employ. This will assist you with the recruitment of the right person:

HOW DO I SET UP MY BUSINESS?

Now that we've looked at the different business advisors that you may need, we need to consider how best to set the business up. You may have heard of limited companies, partnerships and other business formats, but there is a wide range open to you, and it is worth considering carefully which format would be best from both a commercial and a taxation perspective.

Sole traders

Possibly the simplest kind of business to run, a sole trader (otherwise known as a sole proprietorship) is a business that is owned by one individual, and from a legal perspective there is no difference between the business and the individual – this is explained in greater depth in the Limited Company section.

A sole trader business can be set up very easily, and only requires minimal form filling to be registered with HM Revenue & Customs. There is no other form filling required, and no requirement to file accounts publicly, so discretion about the businesses finances is achieved.

Sole traders are referred to by their proprietor's name, and will usually adopt a trading name, such as the following:

Mrs Smith trading as (or t/a) Yummy Cake Shop

There is no protection over the company name, and if it isn't trademarked there is every chance that another business could use the same name.

Financially, sole traders have some disadvantages when compared to limited companies (at the time of writing). Firstly, as they are legally considered to have no difference from their owner, the individual would be deemed liable for any business debts, and indeed a business failure could well result in personal bankruptcy.

They also have a different tax treatment to limited companies, in that the entirety of the profit of the business is deemed to be the income of the proprietor for income tax purposes. This is explored further in Chapter 7, however in brief the National Insurance that is charged on sole trader profits makes the overall tax burden larger than that of a limited company.

Partnerships

Partnerships are a combination of more than one trader, and are similar to sole traders except they are owned and operated by more than one person. The partnership would normally have a partnership agreement, which is a legal contract between the business partners about how the business will conduct its day-to-day activities, and also how the partners will deal with any disputes should they arise in the future. If a partnership agreement is not prepared, and no agreement is implied, it is presumed that the terms within the Partnership Act 1890 apply.

Like a sole trader, a partnership is not required to register anywhere except with HM Revenue & Customs, so the startup costs are minimal. They have the same naming situation as sole traders as well, so a typical partnership name may be:

Mrs Smith & Mr Jones trading as Yummy Cake Shop

Partnerships have the notion of joint and several liability, as the partnership is deemed to simply be an extension of the individual partners from a legal perspective. As such, there is a risk to all partners in the partnership should the business incur debt. Partnerships are more often used for larger businesses than sole traders, and traditionally were used for professional businesses such as architects, doctors' surgeries, accountants and solicitors.

Private Limited Companies

Although a limited company sounds daunting to those with no experience of running one, they are the most common choice of business vehicle for startups. From a legal perspective, they are seen as being a *separate legal entity* from the owner(s), and as such can incur debt and own assets in their own right. They also can enter into contracts in their own right, as if they are a 'person'.

A limited company is formed at Companies House, and would have its own unique company number and name. No other companies are allowed to use the name of an existing company, and there are also sensitive words that are protected from use. So for example, the Yummy Cake Shop as mentioned above would become:

Yummy Cake Shop Limited (or Ltd)

A private limited company is run by its directors, who may or may not be the same people as the shareholders (owners). Some companies are set up with the intention of being not-for-profit, and are known as companies *limited by guarantee*. More commonly for startups, the company is set up as a company *limited by share capital*. These companies are often formed for the tax advantages that arise from effective remuneration strategies, and also the commercial advantages of being seen to be a registered limited company.

Limited companies do however have two main disadvantages, in that firstly they are required to file details of their financial performance and their governance publicly, and secondly that there is a large administrative burden in the additional requirements of Companies House and the Companies Act.

Limited Liability Partnership

Limited Liability Partnerships are a relatively new business structure, introduced in the Limited Liability Partnerships Act 2000. The best way to describe a limited liability partnership (LLP) is as a hybrid between a limited company and a traditional partnership.

Just as with a limited company, a limited liability partnership is formed at Companies House, with its own registration number and unique name. Again, using the Yummy Cake Shop example, a limited liability partnership would be known as:

Yummy Cake Shop LLP

The limited liability partnership would be under the same naming restrictions as a limited company (PLC). Again, as with a limited company, it is a separate legal entity in its own right, and can enter into contracts as a legal person. The difference is that a limited liability partnership is made up of members who are much like partners in a partnership. Each limited liability partnership has two *designated members* who are required to file the accounts for the partnership and to sign the accounts.

Each partner is taxed in the same way as a partner in a partnership, and for VAT purposes the limited liability partnership is deemed to be a partnership, despite being a separate legal entity. There has recently been some legislation passed which puts an additional taxation burden on members who are deemed by HM Revenue & Customs to actually be 'employees'.

Public limited companies

Although rare, it is possible for a startup to commence trading as a public limited company (PLC). They are the same as private limited companies (above), however the shares in a public limited company may be freely sold and traded to the public. There is no requirement for a public limited company to be listed on a stock market, although to be floated on a stock market such as AIM, you would need to be a PLC.

Each PLC must have a minimum share capital of £50,000, of which one quarter (£12,500) must be paid up. Therefore there is a much higher financial commitment from the founders of a PLC when compared to a private limited company. They also have additional reporting requirements when compared to a private limited company. The naming convention again is in line with private limited companies and limited liability partnerships, with the abbreviation PLC used at the end of a company name:

Yummy Cake Shop PLC

OTHER BUSINESS FORMATS

The above are the typical business formats that a startup would use, however there are some other business formats that may be appropriate, such as Community Interest Companies and Limited Partnerships. It is important that you take professional advice regarding all of the options open to you before setting up your business.

PRACTICAL STEPS THAT YOU NEED TO TAKE

Now that you have an idea of the various business structures available to you, you can start to make some steps towards establishing yourself in business, and if necessary creating the legal structure for you to operate the business from. I would suggest that at this stage, it is inappropriate to spend too much money on professional advice until you have performed the basic market research and have prepared some of the business plan, as this will give you a more critical appraisal of the business.

Setting up a limited company at Companies House can now be done online, at very low cost; however it would be worth consulting with your professional advisors during the free of charge consultation to establish whether they believe that any specialist input is required for the formation of your business. These may include ideas for tax or commercial reasons surrounding share structures, and the company's statutory documents.

Depending on the nature of your business, you may also be required to register with a regulatory body, such as ABTA (the Association of British Travel Agents), or FCA (the Financial Conduct Authority). At this stage it is worth reviewing the membership requirements of any such associations or trade bodies, to find out the following:

- **Financial requirements.** Do they require you to have a certain level of capital?
- **Operational requirements.** Is there a code of ethics that you have to adhere to?
- **Mandatory membership.** Do you need membership to trade or is it just desirable?
- **Membership benefits.** Does membership solely allow you to trade, or are there added benefits to becoming a member?

→ NEXT STEPS

In this chapter we've looked at who you need on board to make your business a success. Although not all of these types of advisors are essential, it is worth contemplating each one to make sure that you give yourself the greatest possible chance of success in your new business.

We've also run through how to find the advisors, and how to select them. Together with an informal advisory board, you should be well on your way to having a strong team to help you build your business.

Your next steps have to be to take action. Start researching potential advisors, and begin your initial conversations with your prospective team so that you can get advice during the vital business planning stage.

Next, we will be looking at market research and how effective research can give you a competitive advantage in your business.

FURTHER READING

Useful resources:

How to choose an accountant:

http://www.startupdonut.co.uk/startup/tax-and-national-insurance/accounting-and-bookkeeping/q-a-choosing-an-accountant

How to choose a solicitor:

http://www.lawsociety.org.uk/for-the-public/using-a-solicitor/

How to choose a consultant or coach:

http://www.passionforbusiness.com/articles/select-small-business-coach.htm

Companies House:

http://www.companieshouse.gov.uk

TAKEAWAYS

What actions do I need to take to set up my business?

Who are the key advisors that I will need help from?

What questions should I be asking them?

What ideas do I have about the business?

4 MARKET RESEARCH AND UNDERSTANDING THE BUSINESS

✔ IN THIS CHAPTER YOU WILL LEARN

- How to perform market research
- Types of market research
- How to evaluate the results of your research

We've now evaluated both yourself and the business from a broad level, and identified the areas in which you will need support. It's now time to dive into some of the detail of the business, and perhaps the biggest thing that you need to understand is how the market for your business looks.

❗ COACH'S TIP

Although once established it's important not to focus too much on where your competitors are going, in the planning stages it is vital that you learn from the things that other businesses in your industry do well, and indeed what can be improved upon.

WHAT IS MARKET RESEARCH?

Market research may seem like a task that only larger businesses would perform; however it is simply the process of gaining an understanding of your competitors. This can be as simple as desk-based internet research, or potentially as in-depth as engaging specialists to perform this work for you.

If you have already worked in the industry that you are looking to set up in, it's likely that you already have some informal market research from your experience in the business. In Chapter 2 (Coaching Session 9), we looked at the initial perceptions that you have of your competition. It would be worthwhile referring back to this at this early stage of market research to refresh your memory of the notes you had made previously.

COACHING SESSION 20

Research the competition

Having reviewed the notes that you made in Coaching Session 9, note the key areas that you feel would warrant further research (this may include competition that you don't know enough about, or unique businesses that you feel you could learn from):

TYPES OF MARKET RESEARCH

As mentioned earlier, market research can range from the obvious to the costly and complicated.

> **! COACH'S TIP**
>
> In my experience, the most effective research is the practical research that you can perform yourself. Although a report from a research agency might tell you the economic contribution of a sector and other such 'big picture' statistics, realistically this information is only of benefit for impressing people with facts and figures – in the day-to-day running of your business, these statistics are irrelevant.

Some of the different types of market research are as follows:

Desk research

With simply an internet connection and a computer, you have far more data at your disposal than ever before. It is possible to perform a huge amount of your market research online, simply by using a search engine to find your competitors. This does have a weakness, in that some sites are optimized for Google and other search engines, and as such those that appear to be main potential competitors may just have a slick image for the internet. Likewise, you may have some very strong competitors who have not fully embraced the internet.

Your potential competitors' websites are only one area of internet research that you can perform. There are also directory sites, industry websites, and potentially discussion forums that you can use to gain more information about the sector and those that operate within it.

Trade journals

Trade magazines and journals are a great resource for anyone looking to break into a sector that is new to them. They will often have commentary from some of the leading figures within the industry, which can provide you with further avenues to research.

Also, there is a very rough estimate you can make of the health of a sector, simply by looking at the amount of advertising that is placed in these journals. Ultimately, advertisers will only pay for their adverts to be printed if there is a willing market to purchase the goods or services. Therefore, if there appears to be a buoyant market for advertising, this normally reflects well on the industry itself. The nature of the journal can also supplement this information. If it is a long-standing journal, perhaps with a range of competition, and still sold in newsagents, this is a stronger sign than a journal in an industry which doesn't have established journal and cannot gather sufficient circulation to justify a prime place on a newsagent's shelf.

Walking the streets

Although in the literal sense this task is more relevant for retail and food operations, there is a wider application of this applicable to all sectors. Take a wander down some local high streets, visit some industry networking events, drive around local industrial estates; any time that you get outside and see what is actually happening in the world is of huge benefit when researching the competition. You might even have the opportunity to start a conversation with the right person, who might give you some nuggets of information about the local economy or the sector.

Questionnaires and footfall analysis

A well-designed questionnaire will allow you to find out information from your target market. I would always suggest that questionnaires are multiple choice, and as brief as possible so that you remove any objections to completing them.

Questionnaires can be posted, face to face, or over the telephone. When performed face to face they can be conducted as part of your local 'walking the streets', and they will allow you to gauge the demographic of your target market (this is particularly important for food and beverage or retail businesses). Footfall analysis is another key tool, which can allow you to project the likely target market simply by counting the number of pedestrians in a particular area.

For footfall analysis to be accurate, you need to perform the checking on a variety of days and times, and also ensure that your projected conversion (i.e. footfall vs visitor rate) is reasonably accurate. This can be measured by observing your competition's footfall and visitor rate.

Performing footfall analysis is extremely simple, and just requires a notepad, a clicker (available online), warm clothing and patience!

Industry associations

Industry associations are a great way of getting to know your fellow business owners and managers in your sector, and the informal networking that can happen at these trade events will lead to you finding out more about the current trends in the sector. As a startup, you might have difficulty joining these associations as a full member until you have had sufficient trading experience; however it is always worth asking if you can attend an event or two as a guest – remember, you are a potential 'customer' of the association!

These associations also tend to have trade journals. Although these are often simply based on press releases from their members, they can again provide you with a wealth of knowledge about your competitors.

Local knowledge and professional advisors

There is a wide range of information that your existing contacts know, and all you need to do is ask them! Depending on how you selected your professional advisors in Chapter 3, you may find that they either know your sector or your local market. Try having conversations with other contacts that you have, this will allow you to pick their brains and gauge their feedback on your potential competition.

Focus groups

Often, a business has a unique slant on an existing product or service. A way to research what your potential customers may think, and to receive feedback, is to conduct a focus group meeting.

Prototype testing

If you are looking at launching a product, it is vital that you actually test the product to ensure that the market has an appetite for it. Prototype testing allows you to do this at a relatively low cost, and can be offered as part of a focus group to allow you to receive group feedback on the product.

Research agencies

If you are looking at starting overseas, or at a new market which is completely unfamiliar to you, there are agencies that can provide you with formal market research data. This data can be sourced from commercial organizations, or alternatively you can consult with UKTI (UK Trade and Investment), a government department which has been set up to assist UK businesses with exporting their goods and services.

COACHING SESSION 21

Sources of data

We will now look at preparing a list of the sources of data for you to use for your market research. List below three different sources of each type of research, to help you construct your action plan for market research:

Desk research (directories, forums, websites, etc.)

Trade journals and magazines (include mailing lists and subscription websites)

Local street research (note specific areas to visit)

Industry associations and key individuals within the sector

Professional advisors and other contacts to speak to

WHAT DATA SHOULD BE OBTAINED?

Now that you have a list of potential sources of data, it's important to decide what information is required to help you formulate your business plan.

Before we look at the details of the different information that you could obtain, it's important that you understand the difference between the two main types of data:

Qualitative data	Quantitative data
Qualitative data is based on descriptions and perception of service. It is based on observations, but cannot be accurately measured. It may include sensory experiences such as the look, feel, smell and taste of an item.	**Quantitative data** is based on numbers, and can always be measured exactly. It may include number, total, time, ages, height, etc. – in fact anything that can be measured.
Example 1 – Data for a coffee from a coffee shop	
<ul><li>Friendly barista</li><li>Calm atmosphere</li><li>Cold coffee</li><li>Frothy but too milky</li><li>Served in a brown mug</li></ul>	<ul><li>1 minute 35 seconds queuing</li><li>Noise level 71 dB</li><li>Price £2.95</li><li>14 choices on the menu</li><li>2 upsell opportunities identified</li></ul>
Example 2 – Data for a bank or building society	
<ul><li>Old-fashioned building</li><li>Polite and professional staff</li><li>Dated décor</li><li>Strong brand image</li><li>Staff seem happy to work there</li></ul>	<ul><li>2,000 square foot building</li><li>Counter protected by XYZ glass</li><li>3% interest rate on savings</li><li>8.4% interest rate on loans</li><li>Established since 1932</li></ul>
Qualitative data focuses on **qualities**	Quantitative data focuses on **quantities**

COACHING SESSION 22

Qualitative or quantitative data

Now that we understand the differences between qualitative and quantitative data, it's time to think about which data would be most relevant for your business. Roughly what split would you be looking to achieve, and why? Which would be harder to obtain?

Examples of qualitative data research

Below are some example questions that you may look to answer about your competitors, which focus on qualitative matters:

1. How well known is the business in the local/industry community?
2. Does the business interact with the local/industry media?
3. Does the business partake in socially responsible/charitable activities?
4. How strong is the brand image of the business?
5. What colours does the business use throughout its corporate branding?
6. Does the business seem modern or antiquated?
7. What emotional feelings do you have about the business?
8. What emotional feelings does the business generate in its customers?
9. What emotional feelings does the business generate in its staff?
10. Does the premises seem to be busy or empty?
11. What types of customer does the business typically attract?
12. How high do you feel that the staff morale is?
13. Is the leadership team effectively managing the business?
14. Does the business seem to be innovative?
15. Does the business feel like it's growing or stagnating?

⚇⚇ COACHING SESSION 23

Qualitative questions

The above list of suggested qualitative questions is by no means comprehensive. Note below the questions that may be appropriate for your market research, together with any others that you can think of:

Qualitative questions *(cont.)*

In my mind, qualitative data is inherently valuable as it can be verified, and is not subject to personal bias in any way. The problem with obtaining qualitative data is that quite often, the data that you'd like to have is not publicly available, and certainly wouldn't be shared with potential competitors!

Bearing this limitation in mind, I've listed some examples of data that you might look to obtain, split between data which is easy to obtain, and data which is desirable but difficult to obtain.

Examples of publicly available information

- historic financial performance (as published by Companies House)
- footfall outside the premises
- length of trading
- retail pricing

Examples of information that is sometimes available

- number of customers
- number of staff
- square footage of premises (if previously advertised by the managing agent on sale)
- rent payable on premises

Examples of information that is hard to obtain

- conversion rates
- breakdown of financial results
- breakdown of marketing spend and marketing activities
- cost of sales

COACHING SESSION 24

Quantitative data

Bearing in mind that quantitative data is often more difficult to obtain, please now make a list of data that you would like to obtain, together with ideas around how to obtain it:

Now that you have prepared a list of both the qualitative and quantitative data that you would like to obtain, together with a list of the sources, it is time to identify which competitors you would like to research.

COACHING SESSION 25

List your competitors

Using the information sources compiled in Coaching Session 21, and the activities generated from this list (such as local exploration), please compile a list of competitors, both local and national, that would warrant further research:

List your competitors *(cont.)*

TIPS FOR PERFORMING COMPETITOR RESEARCH

For your market research to be effective, it's vital that you apply a few key principles to ensure that you get the most benefit from your efforts:

Making research objective

One of the biggest problems with researching competitors is that personal bias can slip into your views, particularly when you consider how there is no way to measure qualitative data. I tend to see this with many business owners, who probably don't even realize that they have some inbuilt bias against certain competitors.

A great example would be a local burger bar, which could be biased against McDonald's because they perceive that there is a difference in the quality of beef used. However, most people looking at McDonald's without bias would agree that it is a fantastic business model, which provides a fit-for-purpose product for its customers, in a cost efficient and rapid manner.

Compare like with like

There is little point researching your competitors if you are not prepared, and do not have a consistent set of data that you would like to achieve from the reviews.

For every business that you research, you should ensure that you have a template research sheet, which would comprise questions based on the data that you have already identified as being required in Coaching Sessions 23 and 24.

Use free of charge (or low-cost) resources

It is possible to pay agencies significant sums to perform your market research for you; however I'm a firm believer that this should be a low-cost activity, as much of the information can be obtained by you with some effort and time.

Make use of resources that are available to you, including Companies House data, data from corporate credit appraisers, pricing information from potential suppliers, and of course the internet. Finally, be sure to use your own eyes and ears – usually the best way to see what is happening in the world of your competitors.

COACHING SESSION 26

Action plan

Now let's create a research action plan. Bearing in mind the above, together with the results from all of your previous Coaching Sessions, write down your next actions (such as set up an account with Companies House, contact suppliers for details of costings, find a friend/mentor to help you objectively review the competitors) and set a deadline for the data from your market research to be collated:

Deadline for completion:

WHAT TO DO WITH THE DATA

Once you have gathered all of this data, you need to find a way to collate it into a format that will allow you to demonstrate to others in your business plan that you have approached this research intelligently, whilst also giving them the key information that they need.

In my experience the best way to approach this is in exactly the same way as for your own business idea. You may recall that in Chapter 2, we explored a well-known model (the SWOT analysis) which we applied to your business in Coaching Session 11. When reviewing business plans for startup businesses, the most comprehensive and well thought out plans also include a SWOT analysis of the business's key competitors, allowing the reader to understand the competitive advantages (and indeed disadvantages) of the business.

! COACH'S TIP

I must reiterate that it is important that this process is approached impartially, as although the business idea will be close to your heart, any users of the business plan would see bias when reading the plan, and one of the main things that anyone reading a business plan is looking for is an honest appraisal of the market and competition.

→ NEXT STEPS

In this chapter you have been walked through the basics of market research. You should have a clear understanding of the different types of data, and some cost-effective methods that you can use to obtain this information.

You should also have a comprehensive list of potential competitors, and an action plan in place for the review of these competitors. Together with a template for comparing these businesses, you should be able now to produce an intelligent appraisal of the market that your business will be competing in, and document the advantages that your business has over its competition.

You will now be able to critically review your own business idea, to ensure that you are positioned in such a way to minimize the risks of your competition taking advantage of any weaknesses, and in turn you will also be able to start thinking about how to promote your business with the key competitive advantages. Next, we'll look at wrapping up this information, together with the Coaching Sessions completed earlier, in a business plan to allow you to attract funding and support from third parties.

FURTHER READING

Useful resources:

Bartkowiak, Judy, *Market Research in a Week* (Teach Yourself) Hodder & Stoughton, 2010

Hague, Paul et al, *Market Research in Practice: A Guide to the Basics* Kogan Page, 2004

gov.uk video on Market Research: https://www.gov.uk/market-research-business

The Market Research Society: https://www.mrs.org.uk/

TAKEAWAYS

What are the strengths and weaknesses of my competitors?

How can I improve my business model to take advantage of these?

WRITING A BUSINESS PLAN

✔ IN THIS CHAPTER YOU WILL LEARN

- What to include in your business plan, section by section
- Do's and don'ts of preparing a business plan
- Where to take advice

We've now established that the business works, having researched the market and understood the basics of how the business should look. It's now time to put together a business plan. Although this may sound like a daunting task, we've actually discussed how to put together a good proportion of the content in the previous chapters.

WHAT IS A BUSINESS PLAN USED FOR?

❗ COACH'S TIP

A business plan is used for a number of reasons, however in my experience most prospective small business owners only prepare them to obtain funding from the bank. I strongly believe that this is the wrong approach, as they are a valuable document for any business owner.

I believe that the business plan is a fantastic tool for exploring the business and your approach to it. It fulfils the purpose of being a strategic plan, but also a vision and an appraisal of the business. The more honestly that this is prepared, the more robust the plan is – and it's not unknown for ideas to change during the preparation of a business plan!

It also provides an excellent accountability tool for you to monitor the progress of the business once you start trading. Within a typical business plan, as detailed later in this chapter, there are a number of financial projections which you can then track actual performance against, to ensure that you are hitting your budgets. Business plans should also identify and quantify the main non-financial KPI (key performance indicators) of the business, which can also be tracked during this process.

> ## COACH'S TIP
>
> Whilst preparing a plan, it is vital that you are as honest as possible during the process. The typical user of a business plan (investor, bank manager, etc.) will be playing devil's advocate, and looking for opportunities to highlight areas where you could have been more prudent, or perhaps have missed a vital business risk. These weaknesses in a plan might damage the overall perception that they have of you as a business owner, and might cause them to investigate further for other discrepancies. Therefore I would always suggest that you provide a fair and balanced view of both the opportunities and the risks.

WHO SHOULD PREPARE A BUSINESS PLAN?

Many people are daunted by the prospect of preparing a business plan, as it is a document that most people would only ever prepare once or twice in their life, if at all.

Although many accountants offer a 'business plan' service, I would strongly recommend against this, and instead simply use them to review a plan prepared by you, and to prepare/review the financial information. It is important that the business plan reflects you and your business, and I believe that it can only work as a self-appraisal exercise if it is prepared by the entrepreneur.

HOW LONG SHOULD A BUSINESS PLAN BE?

A business plan can range from one sheet of A4 through to hundreds of pages, however for a typical startup I expect to see plans of between 15 and 25 pages. This is broadly divided equally between the 'words' and the 'numbers' insofar as content is concerned.

The key for any business plan is to ensure that you can get your point across fully and clearly, whilst not overwhelming the reader with superfluous detail.

There is no standard format for a business plan; however I'd suggest that you choose a common font in a readable size so that it can be viewed on both Macs and PCs. I would also steer clear of using too many different fonts, colours and sizes. They say 'a picture is worth a thousand words', and for a business which is reliant on a visual experience (say retail, or product businesses), a well-placed visual can often communicate your ideas far better than text ever could.

WHAT SHOULD A BUSINESS PLAN INCLUDE?

When planning to produce a business plan, you should remember that there is no fixed structure of a plan – these documents vary from business to business; however there is a level of expectation from the reader of the plan.

Normally, I would expect to see the following areas covered within a business plan:

- executive summary
- business briefing
- market review
- SWOT analysis
- background of the entrepreneur
- funding briefing
- financial information.

Executive summary

Cutting through the technical jargon, the executive summary should be a concise summary of who you are, what the business needs and how you are going to pay it back. This summary prepares the reader for what the plan should include, and provides a 'big picture' reference point for when they have to dive into the detail. It should only be one page long.

An important point of note is that most investors and bank managers receive several business plans each week. They have an obligation to read through the whole plan, and often less is more! Of course you need to ensure that you cover all of the expected points, and raise everything that they need to be aware of; however by being brief where possible, you will make the reader's life a lot easier! As I mentioned earlier, striking the right balance between providing all necessary details and overwhelming the reader is essential.

COACHING SESSION 27

Executive summary

It is almost impossible to write an accurate executive summary without preparing the rest of the plan in detail, and without an action plan about how it will be structured. We will start by collating some notes on what should be included, so that you have a 'mind map' of what should be in each section. Below are some questions to help prompt you:

1. Who are you? Use your elevator pitch for the business from Chapter 2, Coaching Session 8, together with a snapshot of who you are as an entrepreneur. Try to sell yourself in the briefest way possible!

2. What is the business funding requirement? And what is the intention of the business plan? You might not know a precise funding figure yet, an approximate figure would help at this stage. Chapter 6, Raising Finance, explores this in more detail.

You will note that we haven't even considered summarizing business profitability, USPs etc., as these will vary from business to business, and will also be subject to work performed later in the business planning process. List other areas that you feel need to be covered in the executive summary, whilst being conscious of the need to keep it succinct:

Business briefing

This is where you should provide detail of what the business is, how it will operate, which sectors it will operate in, and the highlights of the financial projections. I would tend to cap this to one or two pages, and also include your vision and mission statement (as prepared in Chapter 2).

This section isn't the place to go into any detail about your competitive advantage, however a broad summary of why your business would outperform others would be worth including. Also, any salient experience or knowledge that you have personally would be worth mentioning here.

COACHING SESSION 28

Business briefing

Most of the information that you have already prepared for your mission and vision statement would go in the business briefing, including the actual final statements. You will however have to expand on the key areas of your business, including your market, your employees, your USP, etc. Make notes below of the key areas you'd like to include:

Business briefing *(cont.)*

Market review

In this section, you can use much of the research that was performed in Chapter 4. The reader of the business plan would want to ensure that you have considered all aspects of the marketplace, including competition that isn't as obvious as your direct competitors.

I would expect to see both quantitative and qualitative information in this section, and a clear explanation of what sets the business apart from its competitors in the marketplace.

SWOT analysis

Again, this has already been prepared in Chapter 2. Make sure that you review this before including it, as some of the subsequent market and business research may well have impacted on your assessment of the business.

Background of the entrepreneur

For me, this is one of the key parts of the plan. Although the business is its own entity, it will flourish or fail depending on the skills and qualities that the entrepreneur behind it has.

One of the key things to highlight is transferable experience that you may have. This may be directly linked to the business – for example, if you were employed as an architect and set up your own practice. However it may be that you are entering into a new area, in which case you should highlight the skills that you have acquired previously. These may include:

- sales skills
- team leadership skills
- financial skills
- administration skills.

It is also wise to include a brief CV within the business plan, as many banks request this as part of their process.

Funding briefing

Any potential funder would want to understand how much they are being asked for, and what the return is for them. It would elaborate on the earlier funding narrative, by drilling into the detail of what exactly the funds would be used for (whether initial capital costs or working capital).

A lender would expect to also see consideration of the funding mix, to show how the proposed deal should look. More information on this is included in Chapter 6.

Financial information

This is the part of the plan in which you will evidence the claims made within your previous briefings, and is often the section that startups need advice on. There are a number of components to the financial section, including:

- **Projected profit and loss accounts.** Typically these projections would be prepared on a monthly basis, for the first three years of the business.

- **Projected balance sheets.** Again, these would typically be prepared for the first three years, however depending on the type of business it may be only for quarterly or annual periods rather than monthly.

- **Cash flow projections.** These would be required on a monthly basis, demonstrating the cash flows of the business.

One common mistake that many new business owners make is not understanding the difference between cash flow forecasts and profit and loss forecasts. When trading in business, there are a number of 'non-cash' items that need to be included within the financial information of the business, such as depreciation. There are also cash items that might not be reflected within the profit and loss of the company, such as capital investment. In Chapter 7, Managing Your Business Finances, we will explore these items in more detail.

ONLINE RESOURCE

An example of the above projections is available at www.TYCoachbook.com/Startup for you to see how these documents should look.

My strong recommendation for all business owners is to take professional advice on the preparation of the financial information, as this is the area that banks and other funding institutions would look to investigate thoroughly.

COACHING SESSION 29

Action plan

Much of the business plan preparation process is simply a case of action, and making sure that you get on with preparing it. Commit now to some dates for the following key areas to be completed by:

Written sections:

Financial information:

Funding requirements:

Executive summary:

Review and completion:

DO'S AND DON'TS OF WRITING A BUSINESS PLAN

There are some basic rules when it comes to writing a business plan, which can save you a lot of wasted time and embarrassment:

- **DO** write in clear English.
- **DO** make sure that your executive summary is clear and covers all necessary areas.
- **DO** make sure that your plan is provided in both hard copy and PDF formats.
- **DO** make sure that you take professional advice where needed.
- **DON'T** use fancy fonts or overwhelming pictures – the user of the plan wants to get to the point.
- **DON'T** over engineer the plan – most readers want to get the information they need as quickly as possible.
- **DON'T** scrimp on the quality of the final document – use decent quality paper, and make sure that the plan is bound in an adequate fashion.
- **DON'T** abdicate responsibility for your plan, it is essential that you have some input into the document so that you can talk about it credibly, and so that you have reassurance that the plan is realistic.

WHERE TO GET ADVICE ON BUSINESS PLANS

Preparing a business plan can seem like a solitary job, but there are plenty of resources out there to help you if you need guidance after reading this chapter.

Bank manager

Although you will be approaching the bank manager with your business plan, often the banks have template plans to give you some guidance as to how they should be prepared. Make sure that you speak to your manager during the process of applying for funding. They have a vested interest in providing funding, as it will be likely to make up part of their targets, but also need to ensure that the bank's money is used responsibly.

We'll discuss more about the fund-raising process in the next chapter.

Accountant

A qualified accountant will be able to help you create and validate your financial projections, and can provide input into the best ways to fund your business. You should therefore hire an accountant to at least review the projections that you have made. If an accountant has been used during the preparation of the plan, it would be worth making note of this in the plan so that the banks can have comfort that professional advice has been sought.

Business colleagues

Any friends or colleagues that you may have who are currently in business can often provide you with a useful sounding board for the ideas in your business plan, and can help you by casting a critical eye over the draft document before you finalize it.

If they are commercially minded, their help would be especially valuable in reviewing the competitor analysis and your unique selling points. Ideally, you'd ask them to take the role of a bank manager, to see if they would lend you money based on the strength of your plan.

Online guides

There is also a plethora of online guides out there to help you build a business plan. A great resource is www.bplans.co.uk, which provides a range of business plan templates to help you get started. You will also find a fantastic resource on http://www.greatbusiness.gov.uk/the-how-to-write-a-business-plan-guide/, which consolidates the various sources of business plan templates, and articles / checklists from the banks and other useful organizations.

☺☺ COACHING SESSION 30

Advice

Now that you know a few sources of information to help you pull your plan together, make a note of who would be best to speak to, together with committed dates to commence these actions / perform research:

➡ NEXT STEPS

In this chapter you have been walked through the main components of a business plan. Much of this is a consolidation of information that we have already prepared in earlier chapters. We've discussed what information should be included, and the best way to present it. We've also covered some key 'dos and don'ts', so that you have the best chance of your plan impressing its users.

During the chapter we've also looked at who can help you with the preparation of a business plan. Undertaking the preparation of a business plan is a huge task, and it is one that I strongly believe should be owned by the entrepreneur, however input from various professionals can help prevent you from making some fundamental mistakes which might affect your chances of obtaining funding.

Once your plan is complete it pays to review and re-review it, to make sure that it reads correctly and that all of the data ties up together – you'll be surprised at just how many plans refer to a figure in an appendix, which doesn't actually appear in the appendix!

You should always bear in mind that the business plan is an organic document. Although it is usually prepared at the outset of the business, I believe that there is huge value in monitoring your actual performance against your plans, and also in revising the business plan periodically so that you always have a structured approach to your business's growth.

Next, we'll be looking at how to raise funding for your business. We'll explore the various sources of funding, and will also look at the practicalities of the process so that you can be best prepared for this.

FURTHER READING

Useful resources

Evans, Vaughan, *The FT Guide to Writing a Business Plan: How to win backing to start up or grow your business*, Financial Times/Prentice Hall, 2011

Tiffany, Paul et al, *Business Plans for Dummies*, HarperAudio, 2007

Consolidated list of business plan information

http://www.greatbusiness.gov.uk/the-how-to-write-a-business-plan-guide/

Online business plan templates:

www.bplans.co.uk

TAKEAWAYS

What steps do I need to take to make my plan a reality?

Who do I need to consult?

Are there any areas from previous chapters that I need to revisit?

6 | RAISING FINANCE

✔ IN THIS CHAPTER YOU WILL LEARN

- What the options are for raising finance
- How much finance can be raised
- How to present your case to potential investors

Now that you have a business plan, you are at the stage where you can consider how best to fund your business, and approach various parties who may be prepared to fund your business. As with the previous chapter, this chapter is very much focused on providing you with information, so that you can consider what would be the best route for you and your business.

Broadly speaking, the funding requirement for any business is split between two areas of financing: working capital funding and capital investment funding. It is important that you understand the different dynamics of both, in order to choose the most appropriate mix of funding for your business. Typically, most business owners consider that their personal bank is the only option to fund their business, however this couldn't be further from the truth.

WHAT FUNDING OPTIONS ARE OUT THERE?

The landscape of funding for businesses has changed dramatically over the last five to ten years. What was a fairly formal, limited market has now expanded with the introduction of crowd funding and peer-to-peer lending. Below are some examples of how businesses can raise the necessary funds:

Personal investment

This is certainly the approach with the least resistance from a lender, however you need to consider whether you have sufficient finances to run the business and maintain a contingency fund should it be required (let's say if the business isn't as successful, or your partner is made redundant, etc.).

> ## ! COACH'S TIP
>
> Even though there is no application process for investing in your own business, or any difficult questions to be answered, I would urge you to ensure that you still go through the process of preparing a comprehensive business plan, to make sure that the business is right for you.

It is always important to make sure that your spouse or partner (if you have one) is as committed to the business as you, and that they are happy to use personal funds if this is the route that you choose. There are very few things that are more frustrating than hearing 'I told you so' after a failed business investment!

Family loans

Family loans are often a popular choice with many startup businesses as there are (usually!) no formal application procedures or credit checks. I would strongly recommend that anyone choosing this route prepares a properly drafted agreement, so that the terms of the loan are clear from the outset. I would also suggest that both sides consider how they will deal with the worst case scenario of the business failing, both financially and personally.

Family loans rarely have a typical structure, and I've seen cases of both interest and non-interest bearing loans, with a range of repayment deals. Regardless of how the loan looks, and regardless of how well you get along with each other at the moment, it is vital that the loan is documented to protect both sides.

Bank loans

Despite the generally gloomy news that the media circulate, all high street banks are willing to lend money to startups. In fact, it's easy to forget that lending money is one of the reasons that they are in business!

Even though there is money to lend, and a variety of government and bank-led initiatives (such as Funding for Lending, Enterprise Finance Guarantee Scheme, and various industry funds), it's important to approach the bank in a professional and knowledgeable fashion. Make sure that you fully understand the detail of your business plan, and can answer any questions confidently and consistently.

As a rule of thumb at the time of publishing, banks will typically meet 50 per cent of the funding requirement for a general startup, and some banks in the franchising sector will extend to 70 per cent for a recognized, established franchise. There are usually arrangement fees in addition to interest, and you must also consider any covenants (restrictions and/or requirements) that might be placed on you whilst the facility is in place.

Personal loans/remortgaging

When investigating financing for a business, particularly if it is a smaller scale startup, always consider the option of raising funds personally. Often, the interest rates for an unsecured personal loan are lower than those for a business loan. There are also no arrangement fees, and potentially other perks such as gift vouchers/reward points offered as new customer incentives.

Remortgaging a property is another option for raising funds. The interest is usually lower than that charged on a personal or business loan, and the repayment terms can be far longer. It is vital however to ensure that both you (and your life partner) are happy to put your property up as security for the bank.

Overdrafts

Overdrafts are often used to fund working capital, where a 'floating' facility is needed. There is no formal capital repayment schedule as with structured finance such as a loan; however an overdraft is technically repayable on demand.

Again, as with bank loans there is typically an arrangement fee, calculated as a percentage of the facility, together with an interest charge for the amount of overdraft used within the period. The facility may also be subject to covenants, which are terms that the business must adhere to in order to continue to qualify for the overdraft.

Leasing/hire purchase arrangements

For asset purchases, it is often prudent to consider whether the item can be purchased using a lease or a hire purchase agreement, which is itself secured against the asset.

There are two types of leases – operating leases, and finance leases. They have different accounting treatments, and fundamentally with an operating lease you are merely 'renting' the item, whereas with a finance lease you are 'purchasing' the item. Make sure that you get clarity on the type of lease before entering into any commitment.

Banks will expect you to consider these arrangements when you are looking to fund a startup with capital assets, as it spreads the funding risk for them.

Factoring/invoice discounting

Factoring is often thought of as a 'funder of last resort', however the market has advanced significantly and there are now a number of factoring companies out there, making the market far more competitive. All of these companies effectively provide funding against your sales invoices, reducing the payment terms dramatically for many businesses. These facilities do however come at a cost, and it can be a more expensive method of financing your business.

You will also need to consider whether you would be best suited for factoring, or for invoice discounting. Invoice discounting services simply provide the financing, whereas factoring companies manage your sales ledger on your behalf. In either case, the ultimate responsibility for bad debts lies with you. There is insurance available against these bad debts, should you wish to mitigate this risk.

Peer-to-peer lending

Peer-to-peer lending is a relatively new way to access finance, facilitated by websites such as Zopa. It allows members of the general public to invest their money into these loans, acting as a brokerage (much in the same way that Betfair adapted the traditional bookmaker's model by allowing customers to bet for and lay against each side). The broker will typically take a lending fee, which is deducted from the interest rate charged by the lender to the business.

This is a funding avenue that is open to most individuals with a good credit history, and this market is developing at a rapid rate. As it is a new approach, there haven't been too many horror stories in the press about peer-to-peer lending, however this might change as the market develops.

External seed funding

External funding is often confused with angel investment/venture capital, and although some angel investors/VCs might offer seed funding, it is important to differentiate these when considering funding strategies for your business.

Typically, a seed-funding round would be in exchange for equity, and because of the inherent risk of a startup, often the valuation can look extremely low from the entrepreneur's perspective. It's vital to remember that this is probably one of the riskier personal investment strategies from the investor's perspective, as they may have little or no involvement in the business, and hence no control of the destiny of their investment.

When entering into such an arrangement, it's vital to agree on the key terms of the deal, including whether the investor's capital is repayable in any way, whether there is to be any 'salary' for the entrepreneur before the profit is divided, and the general nature of day-to-day conduct between investor and entrepreneur. It's also wise to agree on a structured exit strategy, with a pre-determined valuation mechanism, so that both parties have certainty of how the relationship will finish.

If you do consider seed investment, make sure that you take professional advice so that the investment can qualify for any relevant tax reliefs from the investor's perspective, which will make the deal more attractive for them. Also be sure to take advice on the structure of the deal from a corporate finance expert, to prevent it from causing problems down the line if subsequent angel/venture capital funding is your intention.

'Sweat equity'

An arrangement that I often see is that an entrepreneur with a concept for a company that requires some coding for example, will approach a coder and offer him a slice of equity in the company in return for his efforts in coding the software.

This arrangement works well in theory, but in practice there are a number of potential pitfalls to consider. By thinking carefully about the deal that is offered, and treating it as any other investment, you can avoid these. Make sure that you place a value for the efforts being put in by the other party, including a proportion for risk, and compare it against the value of your business.

> ## ! COACH'S TIP
>
> Consider whether an exit strategy for the other party is necessary. Make sure that you have a shareholders' agreement, detailing the structure of the deal, in place. Finally, think very carefully about whether a formal funding facility would prove to be more cost effective for the company long term.

Crowd funding

Similar to peer-to-peer lending, crowd funding is another relatively new method of funding businesses, particularly startups. Various websites such as Kickstarter and Crowd Cube have popularized this avenue for funding, and there have been a number of successful fundings through these sites.

For a business to be successful in raising funds in this route, it is important to decide whether you will raise funds on the back of a promotion (such as seen on Kickstarter) or by issuing an equity share to the fund. Many businesses, particularly those producing gadgets, have been able to fill their order books by offering their products for a discount, together with limited edition 'early bird' versions for the early adopters at a premium price. These pre-orders have enabled them to raise their funding requirements without giving away any equity whatsoever.

Not all businesses are as glamorous as some of the innovative technology companies, and as such a share of equity might be a necessary evil to raise the necessary funds.

Angel investment/venture capital

Before we dive into the details of the differences between angel investment and venture capital, I would firstly comment that despite being asked about these routes by most new entrepreneurs, they are not relevant (and indeed the lenders are not interested) in most new startups!

Angel investors and venture capital firms typically help businesses by providing capital, and board level input, into businesses. The differences between a venture capitalist and an angel lie in the level of funding provided (most angels wouldn't consider a deal under £100,000, whereas a venture capital firm would need the deal to be significantly higher), and the structure of the deal (the angel might well be a personal high net-worth investor, whereas VC investment normally comes from a dedicated fund).

If you believe that your business truly requires seed funding, followed by angel/ VC investment, it is essential that you take professional advice at the outset to put together an investment strategy so that your early funding decisions do not put your subsequent plans at risk.

COACHING SESSION 31

Funding

Although the above may seem like a lot of information to digest, in reality it is only a snapshot of the various funding options out there, as each type of funding could justify a book in its own right!

Given the information above, what types of funding could be suitable for your business?

COACH'S TIP

A question that I'm often asked is how much can be raised. Unfortunately, the answer is often 'how long is a piece of string?'! The amount that can be raised depends on the type of funding, the type of business, and the industry that it is in. Taking a step back from the details, ultimately any funder is simply looking for debt that can be serviced and repaid within their criteria, with an interest rate to match the risk and required return for them.

Usually, I find that banks will match the level of commitment from the entrepreneur, and with recognized franchises they will extend their financing to 70 per cent of the total investment. Ultimately, we always need to come back to establishing what is actually required to start the business and operate for the initial period of trading, until the business becomes self-sufficient.

COACHING SESSION 32

How much funding?

Let's now explore the funding requirement for the business. This is unlikely to be an exact calculation, as there are likely to be timing issues and other matters which can affect how the money is lent. The mix of funding (see below) can also affect how much is needed, and when. But to start with, we can gauge an approximation of what is needed:

1. To start, total any capital commitments that you will have before you start, such as assets, stock, vehicles, etc.
2. Now consider your initial promotional activity – roughly how much will you need to get the business off the ground?
3. Are there any deposits, etc., that you will need to pay? This might be for a rental premises, or for hired equipment.
4. Now we need to consider your working capital needs. It's likely that your cash flow projections prepared previously had a deficit in some months. What was the maximum cumulative deficit (in other words, the largest 'overdraft' position)?
5. Finally, add any professional services that you will require in the early days – items such as legal advice, accountancy advice, or consultancy.

1. Capital commitments:

2. Promotional activity:

3. Deposits:

4. Working capital:

5. Professional services:

Total Funding Requirement (1+2+3+4+5):

Now that you have considered the total funding requirement, it is worth looking at the overall funding mix to spread the risk of the funding as much as possible. In theory, the total funding requirement calculated in Coaching Session 32 is the maximum that you would approach the bank for, and by carefully reviewing each area you can reduce the amount of a total loan, which in turn will make the deal more attractive for the bank.

The first step is to look at whether there are any assets (included in section 1) that can be financed by a lease or hire purchase agreement. Although the effective cost of financing might be higher than a loan, financing assets through a leasing company means that 100 per cent of the value is financed, reducing the potential personal investment from you. It also reduces the loan amount required, meaning that the proposition should be stronger for the lender. Bear in mind however that the assets will be secured, and can potentially be recovered should the lease or finance commitments not be met.

You can then consider whether any part of the funding should be provided as an overdraft rather than a loan. In particular, the working capital requirements might be more suitably financed as an overdraft, due to the day-to-day changes in requirements. Rather than commit to financing the whole amount at day one, an overdraft facility might be more cost effective for the business.

There may also be timing to consider, if not all funds are required on day one. Consider whether there is a case to be put to the bank for separate tranches of financing.

COACHING SESSION 33

A funding mix

Clearly, striking the right funding mix is essential for obtaining funding. We explored potential options in Coaching Session 31 – now, consider in more detail at how the various aspects can be funded:

Probably the most nerve-wracking part of the whole process of starting a business is pitching the business to funders – in part due to television programmes such as *Dragon's Den*. In reality, although you must expect your ideas to come under scrutiny, the actual meetings with bank managers or funding organizations will be more relaxed, without the formal pitches, and will be a two-way process.

There are however some ground rules that you must be aware of. Firstly, it is vital that you know your business, and your business plan, inside out. They will expect you to have a grasp on the financials of the business, and to understand exactly what makes money and what the potential warning signs are.

They will also expect transparency and honesty from you. If there is a major weakness in your business, for example a strong competitor or a technological advance that you are not prepared for, you should be honest about this, and explain how you would look to overcome this weakness.

Since the credit crunch, there have been changes in how the banks are set up, and how they motivate their teams. There are also more modern banks which purport to have local decision-making authority, and are aimed to help small businesses. In general however, you would expect the following process:

1. Meet with a local bank manager – the level of the banker will depend on the plans of the business. (Banks are often divided into small business, commercial, and corporate levels, and the managers in each level are specialists in businesses of that size.)

2. Once the plan is prepared and the pitch made, the bank manager will review the plan, suggest amendments and make a proposal to the underwriter, together with a case highlighting their support of the plan.

3. The underwriter will reply with a decision.

Although I have no experience of working within a banking team, I understand from my contacts at a couple of banks that bank managers are now required to co-sign decisions along with the underwriters. This means that they are truly acting on behalf of the bank, as they are now responsible for the lending decision, rather than just acting on behalf of the business. Therefore it is more important than ever to make sure that you prepare your approach carefully, and conduct all negotiations professionally.

→ NEXT STEPS

In this chapter we have looked at the various funding options available to startup businesses. As you have seen, there are a number of routes available to aspiring business owners and because of this, you need to make sure that you choose the route that is right for you and your business.

We've also performed a couple of exercises to gauge a ball-park investment level, and to see what routes could potentially work for your business. These will be refined down the line as you prepare your actual cash flow projections, as you will have more of an understanding of your maximum projected deficit.

One of the things to bear in mind is that all funders will approach the funding conversations with you as if it is their own money, even if they are only an employee of a bank. So, if there is a more suitable way to fund your business (for example, leasing equipment rather than bank overdraft), you should expect to be told this. Simply put, they wouldn't want to lend their own money if they have any doubt about repayment, and would look for risk to be shared wherever possible.

Next, we'll be looking at how to raise funding for your business. We'll explore the various sources of funding, and will also look at the practicalities of the process so that you can be best prepared for this.

FURTHER READING

Useful resources:

Berkery, Dermot, *Raising Venture Capital for the Serious Entrepreneur*, McGraw-Hill Professional, 2007

General guides:

http://startups.co.uk/raising-finance/

http://www.smallbusiness.co.uk/starting-a-business/start-up-funding/

Venture capital guide:

http://www.bothsidesofthetable.com/

👍 TAKEAWAYS

What steps do I need to take to firm up my funding plan?

Who do I need to consult?

Are there any areas that would benefit from further study?

Are there any areas from previous chapters that I need to revisit?

7 MANAGING YOUR BUSINESS FINANCES

✔ IN THIS CHAPTER YOU WILL LEARN

- How to effectively manage your finances within the business
- How to understand the financial reports that your accountant will give you
- How to improve the cash flow within your business

Now that you have fully planned out your business, and established how funding can be structured, it's time to move into the next section of this workbook and look at the day-to-day running of the business.

As mentioned earlier, this section of the book covers the activities that you will have to handle day-to-day in your business. A lot of this information isn't immediately obvious, and many business owners are surprised by the wide range of duties that they are expected to ensure are covered.

MANAGING YOUR BUSINESSES FINANCES

One of the key tasks as a new business owner is making sure that you manage your finances well. Often, a startup is run on a minimal budget, and as such effective cash flow management is key. You don't need to be an accountant to manage your cash position, but you do need to be aware of some key statistics within your business to ensure that a downward trend doesn't leave you with more month than money!

There is an often repeated phrase in business, which you might have heard before:

Turnover is Vanity

Profit is Sanity

but Cash is King

This saying highlights a key area that some new business owners forget: ultimately, your staff, suppliers and landlord will need paying, and cash is vital for the health of a business.

One of the first areas that business owners get confused about when it comes to financial matters is the difference between cash flow and profit. Did you know that a business could have £150,000 profit on paper, but be overdrawn with their bank and struggle with cash flow? Once you have an understanding of the differences, it is obvious, however many entrepreneurs don't immediately understand this area.

There are a number of items that may be included within a profit and loss account that may not be directly reflected in your bank account. If you make a trade sale to another business, it would often have payment terms attached, and as such you might have to wait 30 days to get paid. Similarly, you would have payment terms on your purchases once you are an established business, and again your bank account wouldn't reflect these expenses until the payment is made.

It's vital that you get a grasp on your banking position, and make sure that this reconciles back to your original cash flow projections that you have prepared in your business plan. This will allow you to identify any trends that need addressing early, and also will help you make sure that you are on track. Projections are at best educated guesswork, and as such it could very well be the case that you have budgeted incorrectly. The only way that you will know this is by keeping track of your finances to ensure that you are reasonably close to your original cash flow projections, or performing better than expected.

There are a wide range of ways to manage a startup business's finances, such as:

- **Manual bookkeeping**. It is possible to satisfy HM Revenue & Customs by simply maintaining a cashbook of your income and expenditure periodically. This has become far less common over the past few years, as adoption of computerized systems has increased. The main issue with managing your finances in this way is that reporting is very time consuming, and there is a large risk of arithmetical errors.

- **Excel spreadsheets**. Many businesses that once used manual cashbooks have replicated these systems onto a spreadsheet. Although this allows you to put in formulae to add up columns and rows, it is far more difficult to report on the figures using Excel, particularly if you are not proficient with spreadsheet usage.

- **Desktop software**. I've used the term 'desktop' to denote any software package that is installed onto a PC or Mac, such as Sage or Quickbooks. Typically these packages cost between £100 and £500, and are available as an online download or at any software shop. They allow you to keep a full record of your banking activity, your sales ledger, and your purchase ledger; and often also allow you to raise invoices and track any stock that you may hold. These packages also give you a range of reporting functions, such as actual performance vs budget, profit and loss accounts, balance sheets and detailed reports of creditors/debtors.

- **Online software.** Recently, there has been a shift towards online accounting, with packages such as Xero and Quickbooks Online taking the early lead. They are offered as a monthly subscription, typically for £10–30, and provide you with access to your financial information on any computer, anywhere in the world. These packages allow you to use your time more effectively, as you do not need to be chained to a desk to process your bookkeeping, and often integrate with other packages such as CRM systems so that you can minimize your time spent bookkeeping. These packages can also allow you to use a 'bank feed', meaning that your banking transactions are automatically imported into the software. It seems apparent that most desktop packages are migrating to an online platform, and as such this is the route that I suggest for most new businesses.

COACHING SESSION 34

The right software

It's important that you select a package that your accountant can work with, your bookkeeper (if you choose to have one) can work with, and most importantly that you can work with. Take particular care to make sure that it can provide the reports that you would like, and that it is user friendly. Also, check online user reviews. Use the space below to make notes of the research that you have performed, together with consultation with your professional advisors:

Software recommended by accountant:

Software recommended by bookkeeper:

Notes about the above, together with any other packages identified by web research and / or recommendation:

Once you have identified one or two packages that you feel may be suitable for your business, you should then decide how best to purchase the software and how to get trained on it. Most accountants and bookkeepers get discounted versions of software by being members of partner programs offered by the software houses. So, it's worth negotiating to see if you can get a discount passed on by them, or instead whether they can bundle the licence cost into their fees if it will save them time.

> ## ❗ COACH'S TIP
>
> Lack of training in record keeping is a particular issue that I see with many businesses, and often a relatively low investment of both money and time in the early days will save you significant accountancy bills should your records not be accurate and reconciled.

Do some research about both generic bookkeeping courses, and one-to-one training (often provided by accountants) to see what works best for you. Usually, I find that the best programme of training includes an initial training session with actual data, perhaps one month into trading, together with a follow-up session two months later to ensure that you are on track with your bookkeeping. This way, you can get an 'all clear' from your accountant, and then ensure that there should be no additional costs when it comes to the year end.

The types of reports that you would expect to understand are the following:

Profit and loss account

This report details all income and expenditure in the business, from an accounting perspective. Therefore it doesn't include capital expenses such as the cost of fixed assets, or your original investment. This report is usually prepared for a period of time, such as a specific month or a financial year, and it will show the net profit of your business at the bottom of the page (hence why it is referred to colloquially as the 'bottom line').

There are a number of 'key performance indicators' (KPI) that you should monitor within your profit and loss account, such as:

- **Turnover**. This is the value of sales (before VAT) during the period.

- **Gross profit percentage**. This is the profit that you make after deducting 'direct costs' (costs attributable directly to sales, such as product purchases). It is this percentage that you should monitor carefully if you sell products or have any other costs closely tied to your sales, as a small change in the percentage can lead to a large change in your net profit.

- **Overheads**. These are displayed in the profit and loss account below the gross profit. Each business has different overheads that require monitoring.

- **Net profit**. Ultimately, this is the amount that the business is making, and your tax bill and the end company valuation will depend on the profitability of the business.

These KPIs are the immediately obvious items that you need to monitor, however it is also important to acknowledge the KPIs which affect these financial results. For example, if your business depends on telesales, then the number of calls made, and the conversion rates achieved, will directly affect the turnover, and in turn the net profit.

ΩΩ COACHING SESSION 35

Know your KPIs

To effectively manage your business you need to know what KPIs you should be monitoring. Each business has its own unique KPIs. For example, a chain of supermarkets would target itself on sales per square foot, whereas this would be irrelevant for a 'one man band' business. Likewise, the activities that are monitored (which ultimately result in the financial KPIs) would be different – for example, a football coaching business that I have worked with used the number of footballs owned as a measure of their teaching capacity.

1. Which financial KPIs would you need to monitor within your business?

2. Which non-financial KPIs would you need to monitor within your business?

Balance sheet

This report shows a snapshot of the value of the business, based on what it owns (assets) versus what it owes (liabilities). Very simply, this report gives you a 'net worth' which would be the valuation of the business should you decide to close the business and sell all the assets for what they are worth, and repay all the loans and creditors at this point.

The balance sheet will be made up of several components, including:

- **Fixed assets**. These are the assets that the business owns, and broadly speaking the assets which would be held for more than one year (otherwise known as 'capital assets'). These can be split between 'tangible assets', which are assets that you can see and touch (for example motor vehicles, furniture, computers and machinery); and 'intangible assets' such as licences and goodwill.

- **Current assets**. These are assets that are expected to be used within the day-to-day trading of the business. Items that would be included within the current assets section would be cash at bank, petty cash, debtors, and work in progress. There would also usually be an adjustment for 'prepayments', which is an accounting adjustment to ensure that the financial results reported are in line with what actually happened during the year, rather than based on cash flows (see below – Matching concept).

- **Current liabilities**. These are moneys owed to other people and businesses, that are of a short-term nature (less than one year), or repayable on demand. Such liabilities include bank overdrafts, credit card liabilities, trade creditors and accruals (again, see below – Matching concept).

- **Long-term liabilities**. These are liabilities which have a longer term of repayment, and hence are separated from the more immediate items. These are usually more structured, and might well be secured against an asset of the company.

The above items will give a resulting balance (total assets less total liabilities), which is the net worth of the company, making up the first half of the balance sheet. The intention of any balance sheet is to actually balance – so there is a second half which shows how the net worth is financed (through items such as share capital and retained profit).

Balance sheets are of particular interest to financial institutions as they show the financial health of the business, and allow the reader to determine whether the business has enough 'liquid assets' (current assets less current liabilities) to continue trading.

COACH'S TIP

A key difference that you need to bear in mind when comparing the balance sheet to the profit and loss account is that the balance sheet is simply a 'snapshot' of the business at a single point in time, whereas the profit and loss account is a report on the performance of the business over a period of time.

COACHING SESSION 36

Test yourself

To test your understanding of the basic financial reports that you would expect to get from an accounting system, answer the following questions (delete as appropriate):

1. A profit and loss account is made up <u>on a single date/over a period of time.</u>

2. A balance sheet shows <u>the net worth of the business/the sales of the business.</u>

3. The gross profit margin is calculated <u>after/before</u> business overheads.

4. Non-cash items that do not have a physical payment, such as depreciation, <u>should/should not</u> be included in a profit and loss account.

5. Liquid assets are made up of <u>total assets less total liabilities/current assets less current liabilities/total assets less current liabilities.</u>

Answers for the above Coaching Session are available at the end of this chapter.

MATCHING (ACCRUALS) PRINCIPLE

You will have seen reference to items such as accruals and prepayments within the description of accounting reports. The reason that these adjustments have to take place is that there is an accounting principle of matching, which dictates that accounting reports have to reflect the actual nature of the transactions for the year.

For example, at the end of the year a business might have incurred costs with a supplier that were not invoiced until a month after the period end. According to the matching principle, these costs should be reported against the period (and in turn; the income) to which they relate.

This can also work the other way around – a supplier might invoice in advance of actually providing their service or product; so in turn the financial reports should be adjusted to reflect this.

These adjustments are commonly known as 'cut-off' adjustments, as they do not change the value of income or expenses; merely the period in which they are reported. For most small businesses these adjustments affect the overheads section of the profit and loss account (for items such as insurance and accountancy fees); however for some businesses these adjustments affect their gross profit margin, and as such should be monitored regularly to ensure that they are accurate, and in turn that the gross profit margin is being accurately managed.

MANAGING YOUR CASH FLOW

Fundamentally, the reason that most businesses fail comes down to a cash flow problem – whether it is another business failure that leaves them with a bad debt, a change in market conditions that they can't adapt to quickly enough, or simply their funding being withdrawn, a problem with cash flow can very quickly lead to a business having to close its doors.

Because of this risk, it is vital that all businesses take every step possible to ensure that their cash flow is managed effectively. Here are some tips that might seem simple, but will ensure that you manage your finances effectively to maximize your chance of success:

- **Invoice your customers promptly**. If you do not raise your invoices promptly, you have little chance of getting paid promptly! I have a little rule that I like to apply personally, which is that the value of any work done for a customer goes down for each day that you delay invoicing. What I mean by this is that customers are most enthusiastic about the service or product you provide on the day of purchase. If you then wait two months to invoice them for it, the initial feelings are likely to have disappeared.

- **Make sure you invoice everything you can.** Again, this is another obvious tip, however it surprises me how many businesses I see (in all industries) that do not have a system to ensure that all work done, or all products sold, are actually invoiced. This is perhaps more vital than the first tip – as although a late invoice may get paid, an invoice which is never raised is never paid!

- **Make sure you invoice accurately.** Whilst it is important to ensure that you invoice everything you can, it is also wise not to invoice any more than you should. Not only is this practice unethical and illegal if done on purpose, it will also give the customer an opportunity to dispute the invoice, which will drag out the length of time before you get payment from them. Therefore it is vital that you ensure that you have an accurate invoicing system which can help you avoid errors on invoices.

- **Set appropriate due dates.** Many businesses seem to default to 30-day terms of payment, however I often find that startups adopt these terms with little consideration of the terms that they would like to set. Whilst certain large customers would require you to fit in with their payment policies, it is up to you to determine what your terms of business are. Also, make sure that your accounting system can handle the terms of business that you require, as some software packages can only handle fixed terms of 30 days.

- **Follow up your debtors.** Once you have raised an invoice, and set a due date, it is important to actually chase the debt! Provided that your system can report on it, make sure that you have a regular report of debtors, and have a fixed follow-up process to contact your customers. There are several debt collection agencies who can help you at this stage, and often the introduction of a third party is all you need to get payment from your late-paying customers. Many business owners get worried about chasing debts, due to a fear of upsetting their customers. Keep in mind that a customer who doesn't pay you is usually not worth keeping as a customer!

- **Use free of charge credit from your suppliers.** Having extolled the virtues of effective credit control, it is worth remembering that in turn your suppliers will have payment terms, and you are able to use these to your advantage. If a supplier gives you 30 days credit, try to use this credit as part of the overall funding of your business. I am not suggesting that you perpetually pay late, but do make sure that you take advantage of the permitted credit terms. It is however worthwhile reviewing your suppliers' terms of business to see if there are any opportunities for early settlement discounts, and indeed consider whether it is worth using these yourself on your own invoices.

- **Monitor your bank account regularly.** With online banking, there is no excuse for not knowing exactly where your financial position is every single day. Make sure that you also have a projection of how the upcoming days, weeks and months look, even if only a rough calculation, so that you can take action to improve your cash flow position earlier rather than later.

- **Keep your financiers up to date**. If you do happen to anticipate cash flow difficulties, make sure that you speak to your bankers as early as possible, as they may be able to support you through any difficult times. Your bank has a vested interest in allowing you to continue trading, and provided that you approach them intelligently with a sensible proposal, they would be likely to want to help you through any rough periods with additional facilities. It's important to avoid burying your head in the sand on these matters, as financial support is very difficult to obtain (and usually expensive!) after the event.

- **Stay on top of your tax**. This might seem obvious, but it is vital to make sure that you have sufficient provision for both your personal and corporate taxes – see below.

HOW DO I PREPARE FOR MY TAX BILLS?

> 'In this world nothing can be said to be certain, except death and taxes.
>
> (Benjamin Franklin, *The Works of Benjamin Franklin*, 1817)

As a new business owner it is likely that you are taking the first step into managing your own taxation affairs, as most employees have their employment taxes deducted automatically by their employer through the PAYE system (see Chapter 8 for more information about this, as you may need to operate this for any employees that you take on).

We looked at the different business structures available to a startup in Chapter 3, and the choice of business structure often impacts the taxes that the business will incur in its lifetime. Please note that all tax rates and thresholds quoted below are correct at the time of writing, but are subject to change.

Income tax

Income tax is a personal tax charge, which is levied on employees, sole traders, and investors. At the time of writing, it is charged at the following rates on all trading and employment income above the 'personal allowance' (currently £10,000 for those born after 5 April 1948):

Basic rate (20%)	£0–£31,865
Higher rate (40%)	£31,866–£150,000
Additional rate (45%)	over £150,000

The personal allowance is also reduced by £1 for every £2 of income above £100,000. There are different rates for dividends and savings income, and we'll explore the personal tax position for a limited company shareholder below.

National insurance

National insurance contributions are applied to certain types of earned income to build an individual's entitlement to state benefits such as the state pension, statutory maternity pay and statutory sick pay.

If you are employed, and not a member of a 'contracted out' pension scheme, you will pay a Class 1 contribution of 12% on any income between £153 and £805 per week, and 2% on any income above £805. Your employer will also make a contribution of 13.8% on all income you earn over £153 (with no upper limit).

As a self-employed individual, you would actually pay two different classes of National Insurance – a Class 2 contribution at a flat rate of £2.75 per week, together with a Class 4 contribution of 9% of annual profits between £7,956 and £41,865, and 2% on any profits above £41,865.

As National Insurance is only charged on *earned income*, there is none payable on dividends from a limited company, or bank interest.

Corporation tax

Corporation tax is charged annually on the taxable profits of a limited company at either the small company rate (currently 20% for companies with turnover below £300,000), or the higher rate (currently 21% for companies with turnover over £1.5 million). There is a marginal rate for profits in between these two thresholds, although from April 2015 the intention is for the rates to be consolidated to a single rate of 20%.

Differences between companies/trade

As you can see from the above, there is a variety of taxes that need to be considered, and not all types of taxes are applicable to all types of businesses. For example, a sole trader will only be charged income tax and National Insurance, whereas a shareholder / director of a limited company would also be charged corporation tax.

For many small business owners, it is preferable from an overall taxation perspective to operate as a limited company, and to split the directors' remuneration between wages (operated through the payroll system at a level equivalent to the National Insurance threshold) and dividends. The dividends will attract Income Tax at an effective rate of 25% once the personal income of the shareholder reaches the higher tax rate threshold, however as National Insurance isn't applied to dividends, this is normally an advantageous structure.

> ### ! COACH'S TIP
>
> As mentioned before, not all decisions about business structure should be made based on taxation. It's important that you get independent advice about your circumstances, as there may be other matters that need to be taken into account before a decision is made.

Value Added Tax (VAT)

Value Added Tax (VAT) is known as an 'indirect tax', and is applied to transactions at a headline rate of 20%. There are reduced rates for certain items, and also exemptions and zero rating for items that are considered to be essentials.

Businesses are required to register for VAT if their turnover exceeds £81,000 in any 12-month period, or if turnover is expected to exceed that in the next 30 days alone. Once registered for VAT, a business will have to raise VAT invoices for its customers, and will be required to account for VAT by submitting regular VAT returns.

These returns allow the tax office to see the VAT that you have charged on your supplies (output tax), less the VAT that you have reclaimed on your expenditure (input tax). There is also space for you to declare other financial statistics, such as the total value of sales and purchases. There are a few schemes within the VAT legislation that simplify matters for business owners. As you will see, when it comes to VAT the devil is in the detail, and it's important to obtain guidance.

Cash Accounting

Provided that the turnover of a business is below £1.35 million, a business can use the Cash Accounting Scheme. This allows you to operate your VAT on a cash basis rather than on an invoice basis, protecting you from the cash flow risks of bad debts (in the standard scheme, you would pay the VAT once an invoice is raised, regardless of whether the cash has physically been received – and if the debt turns bad, you would have to claim relief down the line).

You can stay in the scheme until your turnover reaches £1.6 million, and as a general rule of thumb, if the value of your VAT (applicable debtors) is higher than the value of your VAT (applicable creditors) it is worth considering the Cash Accounting Scheme.

Annual Accounting

The Annual Accounting Scheme is available for small businesses, and uses the same thresholds as the Cash Accounting Scheme. By electing to use the Annual Accounting Scheme, you are still required to maintain proper accounting records for VAT purposes, but only have a requirement to file one VAT return per year. You get two months to complete this return (rather than the one month for standard businesses), and have a fixed amount of VAT to pay over instalments with the balance being adjusted on the final payment. The risk of this scheme is that if your turnover decreases, you are committed to the fixed amounts. Also, if your business regularly receives VAT refunds, you will only receive these once per year.

Flat Rate Scheme

The final scheme available for small businesses is the Flat Rate Scheme, and this simplifies the record keeping for businesses with a total turnover below £150,000. Once in the scheme, you use a flat rate of VAT which is a predetermined rate, from a list updated by HM Revenue & Customs every year. This rate is calculated as an estimation based on your industry, and takes into account the expected VAT to be reclaimed by similar businesses. For newly registered businesses, there is also a 1% discount in the first year.

Businesses can stay within the Flat Rate Scheme until their total turnover is over £230,000. Despite having a lower flat rate of VAT, the full rate of 20% must still be included on VAT invoices.

In my experience, many businesses actually make money by being part of the VAT Flat Rate Scheme, particularly if their actual reclaims are lower than the industry average, and as such it is always worth investigating, even if you don't particularly mind the administration burden of the standard scheme.

Other taxes

There may well be other taxes that impact your business, such as import duties and stamp duty. You should be advised about these during your free of charge consultation with an accountant.

→ NEXT STEPS

In this chapter, which has been largely theoretical, you have been walked through the basics of managing your businesses finances. Without doubt, the single biggest cause of business failure is simply down to cash flow difficulties. We've looked at practical ways that you can improve your cash flow, and more importantly we've looked at how you can stay on top of your finances.

The next steps for you are to finalize your choice of accounting software, based on the software that you find most user friendly. This is now a good time to also appoint an accountant, and if you don't already have one a personal financial advisor, so that you can obtain guidance on any matters that may affect you that you have not projected.

It is also important to take advice on your own tax position, to make sure that you fully understand what you need to put aside, and how to operate in a tax efficient manner.

Bearing in mind the accounting principles that we have explored within this chapter, it would also be wise to review the financial projections that have been prepared originally, to check that they still seem appropriate – paying particular attention to the timing of the cash flows in the business.

Next, we will look at managing people, including the practical and legal obligations that you will need to adhere to as an employer.

ANSWERS TO COACHING SESSION 36

1. A profit and loss account is made up <u>on a single date</u>.

2. A balance sheet shows <u>the net worth of the business</u>.

3. The gross profit margin is calculated <u>before</u> business overheads.

4. Non-cash items that do not have a physical payment, such as depreciation, <u>should</u> be included in a profit and loss account.

5. Liquid assets are made up of <u>current assets less current liabilities</u>.

FURTHER READING

Useful resources:

Collings, Stephen, *Accounting Workbook for Dummies* (UK), Wiley, John & Sons Incorporated; 2013

Mason, Roger, *Bookkeeping and Accounting in a Week* (Teach Yourself) Hodder & Stoughton, 2012

TAKEAWAYS

What are the key numbers that I need to monitor within the business?

How will I manage this process?

What help will I need along the way?

MANAGING PEOPLE

- What aspects of your business require management
- How to deal with other people that will be involved in your startup
- How to stay on the right side of the law

The next area of the business that needs to be managed is the people – your staff, your suppliers, and your customers. Although employing staff may seem a long way off from where you are today, you will need to ensure that you are fully prepared to take on a member of staff, and that you understand the basics of management if you haven't had to perform a management role before.

WHAT PEOPLE DO I NEED IN MY BUSINESS?

To start, we'll take a look at the personnel that you need to employ within your business to service your projected workload. In any business there is broadly a split between the following:

- **Operational Team.** These are the individuals who perform the day-to-day work, including your administration teams, sales staff, marketing staff and technical staff. Their sole responsibility is to carry out the tactics set out by the Tactical Team.

- **Tactical Team.** This is the management team, which might eventually include your sales manager, financial controller, HR manager etc. They set out the tasks and processes for the Operational Team to fulfil, based on the strategy set by the Strategic Team.

- **Strategic Team.** Often the board of directors; however in the case of the typical startup this is usually the entrepreneur! The Strategic Team is responsible for setting the long-term vision of the business.

Whilst this is all well and good in theory, practically we also need to consider what levels of staffing the business can reasonably be expected to support. Staff costs can often be the largest cost of a business, and if the staff are on contracted hourly pay or salaries, their cost is fixed before you take any income for the month. Therefore it's essential to get the balance right before committing to employing anybody, as the most frequent cause of cash burn in a small business is excessive staffing.

ONLINE RESOURCE

An organization chart can help you set out how the business should look. A typical organization chart is available at www.TYCoachbook.com/Startup. It is important to remember that when you create an organization chart, you focus on the roles, not the people that you have in mind.

COACHING SESSION 37

Organization chart

Although you almost certainly will not have the budget to create a fully staffed organization from day one, it's wise to visualize exactly how the business will look by drawing out an organization chart. Start with your leadership (Strategic) team, then consider the roles that will be required in a management capacity. Finish the chart with a breakdown of your operations teams. Bear in mind that more than one role may be fulfilled by each person (not least you!) in the early days.

Strategic

Tactical

Operational

HOW SHOULD I RECRUIT STAFF, AND ON WHAT TERMS?

Once you have an idea of the roles that you need to fill within your business, you then need to decide on the kind of people that you would like to fill these roles, and the nature of their employment with you.

Initially you might find that you have roles within your business which do not justify a full-time employee, yet require specialist skills. Typically these may include IT support, bookkeeping, HR support, and so on. Most businesses look to outsource these roles so that they can have the expertise they require, without the full-time salary attached to it. The relationship with these outsourced suppliers works in much the same way as you would expect when you engage your team of professionals (see Chapter 3, Assembling Your Team).

For other team members, you will need to decide whether you require them on a full-time or part-time basis; whether the role is employed or subcontracted; and whether the role should be salaried or performance based.

Full-time or part-time?

Deciding on whether to employ someone full time or part time comes back to a couple of factors, including the output required from the role; and indeed your budget for staffing. If the role is performance based (see below) this choice isn't so relevant as you will be paying on output, however if it is a salaried/hourly rate role it is vital that you set the correct number of hours from the outset.

Determining the number of hours required from an output perspective is often fairly simple, as the opening hours of your shop, or the chargeable hours required from a staff member, will dictate this. There are however some roles (such as general office administration) which are impossible to quantify at the outset, and indeed have the potential to be expanded by the introduction of unnecessary systems and procedures.

> **! COACH'S TIP**
>
> Look for an employee who is prepared to be flexible, and start with the lowest estimate of hours but with pre-designed systems (see Chapter 9).

Employed or subcontractor?

Generally speaking, this decision is actually taken out of your hands, as HM Revenue & Customs set their own guidelines as to whether somebody is deemed to be employed or self-employed. You can however use their published guidance to help you decide the nature of your working relationship with your team.

As an employer, you would be responsible for deducting PAYE and Employee's National Insurance from your employees' salary. This, together with an Employer's National Insurance contribution, is paid over regularly to HM Revenue & Customs.

You would also be responsible for ensuring that you cover off all employment obligations, such as paid holiday pay, working time regulations, and national minimum wage.

Conversely, when you take on a self-employed individual, they would be responsible for looking after their own tax and National Insurance, and there wouldn't be any employment obligations on your behalf provided that they are deemed to be genuinely self-employed. The self-employment tests are continually refined by HM Revenue & Customs, and you should check out their website at http://www.hmrc.gov.uk to ensure that you are clear on their current approach. As a generalization, they would expect a self-employed individual to be taking business risk, to be in control of their own work, to provide their own tools and equipment, to have the ability to provide a substitute member of staff, and to have no 'mutuality of obligation' with the employer (in other words, they should not expect you to automatically provide them with work, and you should not expect them to automatically turn up for work).

Salaried or performance based?

The final question is whether you would want them to be on a fixed salary, an hourly rate, or some kind of performance-based pay. I am a keen advocate of performance-based pay, as it ties the individual into the business far more than a basic annual salary ever can. Also, by having the basic salary slightly lower than market rate, together with an attractive bonus package, you can create a true win-win arrangement with your employees, whilst minimizing the loss to you should they not perform.

To construct a performance-based package, you need to step back and decide which KPIs (see below) are vital for the role. For example, it would be unfair to target an IT support team member on sales made by the business. You should then also consider whether an overall profit-related pay could be implemented for the team.

COACHING SESSION 38

Identifying roles

Given the roles that you need in your business, now identify your first positions, and the nature of the role (employed/self-employed, salaried/performance, full-time/part-time/outsourced):

Identifying roles (*cont.*)

We touched on KPIs (Key Performance Indicators) earlier, and regardless of whether you decide to pay a fixed salary, or a performance-based pay, it is important that you set the KPIs for each role so that there is a mutual understanding between you and your employee(s) of what is expected from them.

A useful process for setting KPIs in any business is to first look at what are the key components for success across the business. As an example, I would start with the following – bear in mind that not all components would be applicable to all staff:

Key component	Description	Example KPIs
Creating	Generate leads and inbound enquiries	No. of leads Sales pipeline in £
Converting	Sell your products and/or services to these prospective customers	Sales value Conversion rate
Doing	Actually fulfilling the work/ orders that your customers request	Units produced Hours worked
Managing	Overseeing a department, with profit and loss account responsibility	Department profit Staff feedback
Leading	For those in a leadership role, creating a future for the business	Share value Profitability
Delighting	Your performance in the eyes of your customers	Customer satisfaction Repeat orders

COACHING SESSION 39

KPIs

Think of a role within your business, and then some KPIs attached to that role. Not all roles will include all components:

Role:

Creating:

Converting:

Doing:

Managing:

Leading:

Delighting:

WHAT TYPE OF PEOPLE DO YOU WANT?

Another area that requires thought, and possibly some investment, is the profiling of your ideal staff members. As a startup team, you will be working alongside all of your staff, and as such it is vital that you can build a working relationship with them, whilst also making sure that the entire team is balanced.

There are a variety of personality profiling tools available, such as DISC, Myers Briggs, and PROPHET, which will help you to identify a person's behaviours and personality during the recruitment process. You will then be able to match these against your requirements for the role, and the existing profiles within the team. Although these are a useful tool in the recruitment process, please remember that they are only a guide, and can't be used in place of an interview. Often, your own intuition can be more reliable than these tests!

DISC profiling is one of the more common forms of profiling, and allows you to have a rating of an individual's attributes in the following areas:

Dominance

Influence

Stability

Compliance

This is a tool that I've used with my own teams, and through reverse questioning (answering the questions in the way that I'd like an employee too) I've been able to construct an 'ideal' profile for particular roles.

! COACH'S TIP

Something to always bear in mind with these tools is that they can be influenced by an individual's working conditions on a certain day – and indeed are vulnerable to manipulation. There is also an 'internal' DISC and an 'external' DISC, being the true results and those projected to the outside world. In times of stress or pressure, an individual may revert to their 'internal' DISC.

HOW TO FIND STAFF

Once you have decided on the roles that you have available, the job descriptions (covered in the next chapter), how those roles fit into the organization chart, what their objectives are, and the terms of their employment, it's time to start looking for employees.

There are a number of ways of finding staff, and each industry is different. Some will recruit through the Job Centre and local advertising, whilst others will rely solely on agencies or a social networking service such as LinkedIn.

It's important that you don't just rely on the 'tried and tested' methods within your industry, and instead think outside of the box when it comes to recruitment. Ultimately, recruitment is another promotional activity for your business, and if you can find a way of attracting staff in a low cost way, it is solely because you've been able to stand out from other employers.

Some methods of finding staff that are outside the traditional methods of newspapers, the Job Centre and agencies include:

- careers pages within your website
- recruitment open days
- direct headhunting, finding potential staff through, for example, LinkedIn
- registration on online portals for job seekers
- word of mouth
- billboard advertising
- leaflets aimed at your target market
- staff referral schemes.

THE APPLICATION AND INTERVIEW PROCESS

When requesting applications, I would recommend that you have a fixed format for people to use to apply to you; however, choose a format that allows them to demonstrate some creativity or initiative within the application process. A great way of doing this is by requesting an application form (with specific questions that you'd like them to answer), together with a copy of their CV and an application letter.

Some employers even go to the extent of asking for handwritten application letters, so that they can perform handwriting analysis on the letters. I must admit that this isn't a method that I have any experience of myself!

Once you have selected a shortlist of potential employees from your applicants, it's time to commence the interview process. This process doesn't need to simply consist of a face-to-face interview – it may also comprise psychometric testing, aptitude testing, role play, and group activities. It's important for you to consider the right balance of recruitment steps so that you can make sure you recruit the right member of staff, whilst being careful not to put them off applying or continuing the recruitment process.

> **! COACH'S TIP**
>
> The best interviews are approached as a level conversation from both sides, with the candidate exploring whether the business is right for them, in addition to the employer deciding whether to offer a role to the candidate.

Some typical interview questions would be as follows:

Basic questions

- Tell me about yourself?
- What would you say are your strengths and your weaknesses?
- Why do you want this role?
- Where do you see yourself in one/three/five years' time?
- What attracted you to this company?
- What do you like most / least about your current job?
- Why are you leaving your present job?
- Why do you feel you are the right candidate for this role?
- What skills do you feel you can bring to this role?
- What do you know about our industry?
- What experience do you have in respect of your expected duties?
- What experience do you have in managing people?

Behaviour questions

- Tell me about a time that you had to work under pressure?
- Can you describe a time when your work was criticized?
- What typically irritates you about other people, and how do you deal with it?
- What was the most difficult task that you've encountered at work, and how did you deal with it?
- Let's say you had a number of tasks that required completion by the end of the day, and not enough time. How would you approach this situation?
- What was the last project that you managed, and what was the outcome?
- What was the most difficult part of managing that project?
- What was the most difficult decision that you've had to make at work?

- Can you tell me about an occasion when you've gone over and above the call of duty at work?
- Tell me about a time you've had to deal with conflict at work?
- How do you provide negative feedback to people?
- If I asked you to do something that you disagreed with, what would you do?

Personality questions

- How would you describe your working style?
- What kind of work environment are you looking for?
- Do you prefer to work in a structured or entrepreneurial environment? Why?
- Tell me about your proudest achievement?
- What are three positive things your last manager would say about you?
- What are three negative things your last manager would say about you?
- What do you do in your spare time?
- What is your life-long dream?
- What motivates you to get up in the morning?

As mentioned before, the interview should be balanced, and you should expect a good candidate to arrive prepared with some questions for you about the company, and also an understanding of who you are as a business and what you do.

Once the interview has concluded, it is important not to offer the role to somebody straight away, as often emotion (or indeed relief at finding a good candidate) can cloud the overall choice that you need to make. Instead, make a note of the candidate's performance (see below regarding balanced scorecards), and provide feedback to the agency if this is how you have sourced them.

QUESTIONING STYLES

When performing an interview, and planning the questions that you would look to ask a candidate, it is important to understand the difference between open and closed questions.

A closed question is a question which forces the respondent to answer 'yes' or 'no', such as:

Do you like football?

whereas an open question leads the respondent into a more comprehensive answer, such as:

Tell me about your interests outside of work?

You will see that all of the suggested interview questions have been prepared as open questions, to facilitate discussion during the interview.

APPRAISING YOUR CANDIDATES

Once you have interviewed the candidate, you should ideally have a structured method of scoring them. A simple way of doing this is a scorecard, which can be weighted on different areas that you would like to score them on.

For example, you might decide that the following attributes are required from your candidates, with weightings as shown below:

Attribute	Weighting
Role specific skills	9
Management skills	4
Self-sufficiency	7
Presentation	6
Managing conflict	2
Time management	8

◖◗ COACHING SESSION 40

Balanced scorecard

Using the role that you have already decided upon for Coaching Session 39, prepare a scorecard for the required skills, together with a weighting (out of ten) for each attribute.

Balanced scorecard (*cont.*)

Once you have appraised some candidates for a role, it is then very simple to review them by comparing their scores. You simply multiply their score in each area by the weighting, and then total these weighted scores to give an overall rating.

STAYING ON THE RIGHT SIDE OF THE LAW

Employing staff brings responsibilities to the business, both morally and legally. You will now be responsible for the income of another person, and as such there is a framework in place to prevent discrimination and other detrimental actions that you might (possibly inadvertently) cause. As an employer you are also responsible for the deduction of employment taxes, and the administration of certain state benefits such as Statutory Maternity Pay.

National Minimum Wage

The National Minimum Wage is the minimum hourly rate that almost all employees are entitled to by law. It is a criminal offence to pay employees an amount below the National Minimum Wage, and all businesses are required to adhere to the rates shown below:

Year	21 and over	18 to 20	Under 18	Apprentice
2014 (current rate)	£6.50	£5.13	£3.79	£2.73
2013	£6.31	£5.03	£3.72	£2.68
2012	£6.19	£4.98	£3.68	£2.65
2011	£6.08	£4.98	£3.68	£2.60

Working Time Regulations and Annual Holiday Entitlement

As an employer you also have an obligation to ensure that your employees work reasonable hours. The Working Time Regulations were introduced as a result of the EU Working Time Directive. Ordinarily, an employer cannot enforce working hours longer than 48 hours per week, although employees can opt out of that requirement. The opt-out must be voluntary, and in writing. Some jobs are exempted from the regulations, as follows (reproduced from https://www.gov.uk/maximum-weekly-working-hours/weekly-maximum-working-hours-and-opting-out):

- where the working time is not measured and the worker is in control – e.g. managing executives with control over their decisions

- in the armed forces, emergency services and police (in some circumstances)

- in security and surveillance

- as a domestic servant in a private household

- where 24-hour staffing is required
- certain categories of seafarers, sea-fishermen and workers on vessels on inland waterways.

With regards to paid annual leave, almost all employees are entitled to 5.6 weeks (this is known as statutory leave entitlement). For a full-time employee who works 5 days per week, this equates to 28 days (5 multiplied by 5.6). This entitlement includes bank holidays. Part-time employees receive an adjusted amount of holiday, pro-rated (so for example, an individual working 3 days per week would receive 16.8 days – 3 × 5.6). There is a maximum cap of 28 days for those working more than 5 days per week. Employers may choose at their own discretion to offer more paid holiday to their staff. It is also important to remember that employees can accrue holiday leave whilst on maternity, paternity or sick leave.

Health and Safety at Work

As an employer you also have a duty to ensure that your employees are protected from work-related risks. The general duties are set out in the Health and Safety at Work etc Act 1974, and provided that you take reasonable steps to prevent accidents and harm to your employees, you have some protection against claims.

For most small businesses, all that is required is some basic tasks that can protect your staff, which include displaying a health and safety poster, having a first aid box and relevant arrangements, and providing welfare facilities such as hand soap, drinking water and ventilation. Those employing over five staff will also be required to have a formal Health and Safety policy.

Discrimination

Within the Equality Act 2010, there are a number of 'protected characteristics' which have specific protection in the workplace (and indeed in other arenas). It is therefore against the law to discriminate against someone for the following reasons:

- age
- being or becoming a transsexual person
- being married or in a civil partnership
- being pregnant or having a child
- disability
- race (including colour, nationality, ethnicity or national origin)
- religion, belief or lack of religion / belief
- sex
- sexual orientation.

Discrimination can include not hiring someone, selecting a particular person for redundancy, or paying someone less than another person, if it is due to a personal characteristic. Sometimes discrimination can be indirect, if there are working rules or practices that might discriminate against a certain group. As you can see from the types of discrimination, it can occur either during the recruitment process, or during the day-to-day working life of an individual. Therefore you must ensure that your recruitment material and ongoing practices are free from discriminatory elements.

If an employee feels that they have been discriminated against, they can either raise a formal grievance, or take their case to an employment tribunal.

Redundancy

Redundancy is an unfortunate situation where a business has to reduce the size of its workforce, either due to restructuring or for commercial reasons. It is a form of dismissal, and due to the often selective nature of redundancies there is a range of processes that you have to go through as a business owner to ensure that employees are selected fairly. If you reach a point in your business where redundancies may become necessary, the first step should be to take advice from an HR specialist to make sure that you go through the correct routes, hence avoiding potential accusations of unfair selection of staff for redundancy.

When selecting staff for redundancy, it must be based on a fair and objective method of selection, such as time served (last in, first out), voluntary redundancy, disciplinary records, or staff rankings (in appraisals, skills or qualifications). You cannot select someone for redundancy based on the protected characteristics described in the discrimination section of this chapter. Sometimes it is an entire department or business that has to make redundancies, in which case the selection process is irrelevant as the jobs will no longer exist.

Any redundancy process must take place with appropriate consultations and notice periods, and employees are entitled to statutory redundancy pay based on their age and length of service. The need to pay statutory redundancy pay may be removed if you can offer suitable alternative employment to a staff member who is being made redundant.

If the redundancy process isn't followed correctly, or suitable alternative employment isn't offered when it is in fact available, the staff member is potentially able to make a claim to an employment tribunal for unfair dismissal.

Disciplinary processes

Sometimes there are also regrettable situations where you need to take disciplinary action against an employee. Employers should have a written disciplinary policy, and I would suggest that these follow the ACAS code of practice on disciplinary and grievance procedures (available at http://www.acas.org.uk/media/pdf/h/m/ Acas_Code_of_Practice_1_on_disciplinary_and_grievance_procedures.pdf). Although not a legal requirement, following this code of practice will help you ensure that you are following best practice, and will stand you in good stead at an employment tribunal should a case be taken there.

The exact rules of what is and isn't acceptable will vary from business to business, but this may include factors such as behaviour, timekeeping, health and safety, and use of company resources such as the internet. Gross misconduct should also be referred to within your policy, and may include matters such as physical violence, fraud, and theft, which would lead to dismissal without notice. It's important to note that you cannot dismiss someone for a protected characteristic, nor for being a whistle blower.

As this area is a potential minefield for business owners, I would strongly recommend that professional advice is taken from an HR professional should you ever be in the position where dismissal or redundancies are required.

→ NEXT STEPS

This has been a largely theoretical chapter, which has covered a range of employment-related issues. We've looked at what you need to do to select and recruit a staff member, and how to stay on the right side of the law.

To develop this further, I would recommend that you expand on the tasks completed in Coaching Sessions 37–40, and apply them to all job roles identified in Coaching Session 37. This will take some time, however at the end of it you will have a comprehensive range of material to help you in the recruitment of your team members.

FURTHER READING

Useful resources:

Rosenberg, Merrick et al, *Taking Flight!: Master the DISC Styles to Transform Your Career, Your Relationships…Your Life* [publisher and year]

Thompson, Jody, *Why Work Sucks and How to Fix It: The Results-Only Revolution* [publisher and year]

Thompson, Jody, *Why Managing Sucks and How to Fix It: A Results-Only Guide to Taking Control of Work, Not People* [publisher and year]

Cushway, Barry, *The Employer's Handbook 2014-15: An Essential Guide to Employment Law, Personnel Policies and Procedures* [publisher and year]

TAKEAWAYS

What is my action plan for recruitment?

What steps do I need to take?

Are there any areas that I need outside help with?

9 SYSTEMIZING AND SCALING YOUR BUSINESS

✔ IN THIS CHAPTER YOU WILL LEARN

- What the key elements of your business are
- How to structure your business to become as efficient as possible
- How to systemize your processes to allow the business to grow

In Chapter 8 we covered the staffing needs that you will have in the business, and now we will look at the systems that are needed to help the staff work as effectively as possible. I'm a firm believer that staffing and systems should be considered hand in hand, and that *extraordinary systems can allow ordinary staff to perform extraordinary work.*

When considering the systems that are required within a business, you need to establish the key processes within your business. These may differ slightly from business to business, but at a high level most businesses would expect to have the following areas in which they should implement systems:

- Creating, Converting, Doing, Managing, Leading, Delighting

I'm sure that you'll recognize these subheadings from our analysis of staff requirements in Chapter 8.

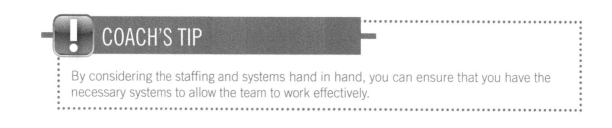

! COACH'S TIP

By considering the staffing and systems hand in hand, you can ensure that you have the necessary systems to allow the team to work effectively.

You almost certainly would have had experience of working with some form of system in your previous employment, whether this was with a large multi-national or a small local business. The first step to being able to establish what systems are needed within a business is to appreciate what a business process is.

A business process is any repetitive task that must take place. This can range from administrative functions, such as answering the telephone or filing, through to managerial and leadership tasks such as board meetings, quality control processes, and staff relationship tasks.

Some example business processes for a finance team could be as follows:

Example: Business processes for a finance team

Recording income and managing customers

- Recording income for the business
- Reconciling income to cash receipts in the till every evening
- Reporting on potential bad debts
- Reporting on outstanding debtors
- Credit control

Making payments to outside suppliers

- Authorizing purchase invoices
- Paying suppliers by cheque
- Recording petty cash transactions
- Reporting on outstanding creditors

Keeping records of all transactions and maintaining records of the finances

- Processing transactions on an accounting system
- Reconciling the bank accounts to ensure completeness
- Processing accounting adjustments (such as depreciation)
- Reporting on financial performance periodically

Appraising business performance

- Comparing actuals to performance in previous period
- Comparing actuals to budget, and an analysis of any variances
- Review of financial KPIs

You can see from the above that there are a number of processes within a section of the 'doing' of the business, which is often undertaken as part of the truly varied role that an entrepreneur adopts when starting a business!

COACHING SESSION 41

Business processes

Based on your experiences so far, review the list below of high-level business sections and identify the functions (as an example, in the Doing, we might have finance, administration, technical support etc.; and in Management we might have staff management, process management…) which will require processes to be established:

Creating

Converting

Doing

Managing

Leading

Delighting

Once you have a list of the functions, you can then analyse the individual tasks for each function to identify where systems may be needed.

WHAT MAKES A GREAT SYSTEM?

For me, the holy grail for any system is one that is idiot proof! Simply put, your aim of systemizing a business should be to eliminate error, fraud, or poor service. There is a fine balance to be achieved here, as on the flip side you need to make sure that you don't over engineer your systems unnecessarily. You have probably heard about the checklist culture that exists in some large corporates and public sector organizations – this can often be detrimental to the main aims of a business as it demotivates staff and hinders efficiency.

! COACH'S TIP

Systems can be as simple as a handwritten set of bullet points of the tasks needed, or far more formal and structured as part of a true operations manual. There are a number of reasons why I often lean towards this approach, which will be discussed later in this chapter.

Example checklist system: purchase invoice authorization and processing

- ☐ On receipt of invoice, scan invoice and file in 'To be authorized' folder
- ☐ Review outstanding invoices and obtain authorization for all invoices from line manager
- ☐ For any invoice over £500, obtain secondary authorization
- ☐ Check arithmetic of invoice and VAT rate/calculations
- ☐ Enter invoice on system and check payment terms
- ☐ Calculate whether there is benefit in redeeming settlement discount
- ☐ Create payment for invoice for last payment run within payment terms

You can see that the above system is likely to be over engineered for a small startup; however for a large corporate these checks are essential to prevent fraud and errors.

COACHING SESSION 42

Identifying systems

Now that you have identified the functions within each business area, please select one and identify the processes that would benefit from systemization:

Business function

Processes that could benefit from systemization:

COACHING SESSION 43

Creating and improving the system

For *one* of the processes above, ideally one that you are familiar with from previous experience, please brainstorm the steps that would require systemization. Use a 'blank canvas' approach rather than merely replicating what you've done before – think about how you can improve on the system, cut out unnecessary steps, and improve efficiency.

CUSTOMER RELATIONSHIP MANAGEMENT

Without customers, you don't have a business, and therefore a vital process that most businesses need to ensure is watertight is customer relationship management.

There are a number of off-the-shelf packages that can help you with this, which range from open source, free of charge products through to enterprise level packages. In my experience the hidden cost is actually within the implementation of these packages – either the cost of consultants to get these systems up and running, or the cost of not setting them up right in the first place!

Effectively, a CRM system will allow you to centrally manage all relationships with your customers, providing centralized visibility of quotations, discussions, relationship management tasks, and ultimately the pipeline of new business that should be generated. They can now also hook up to email marketing systems, accounting systems, EPOS systems and websites to provide a hub for your customers' data.

Whilst these sound very impressive, it is vital to make sure that you only use the systems that you need, as again it is very tempting to over engineer the system so that it includes steps which aren't necessary for your business. A very simple CRM system can be made by simply having customer cards, noting last contact on each card, and filing them in date order by last contact made. You can then simply review the pile of cards regularly and contact prospects from the bottom up!

! COACH'S TIP

Whether the system is computerized, manual, complicated or simple, the key message here is simply to make sure that you have a system to keep in touch with your customers and prospects.

What processes should be included in a customer relationship management system?

Within a computerized CRM system, some of the things I would expect to see are below:

Prospect management

- prospect database
- ability to log conversations and emails
- ability to log expected revenue from customer
- likelihood of conversion (expressed as a percentage)

Marketing process management

- management of marketing campaigns
- ability to group prospects by type / size / industry etc.
- ability to send email marketing campaigns
- ability to track success of marketing campaigns and monitor ROI (return on investment)

Sales process management

- ability to prepare quotations and proposals
- sales process stage management, to quickly identify where you are with a prospect
- ability to monitor sales pipeline value
- ability to monitor conversion rates and sales manager performance

Ongoing relationship management

- systemized approach to regular diarized telephone calls and meetings
- grading of customers based on value and service requirements
- grouping of clients as required
- reporting on performance of relationship managers

COACHING SESSION 44

CRM system

Having read the above examples of what may be included within a CRM system, please note below any other processes that you feel should be included within your CRM system, together with any reports that would be valuable to you:

Processes

Reports

CONSOLIDATING THE BUSINESS SYSTEMS

Once you have considered the various functions in your business, and the processes within each function, you then need to pull together the systems (such as that prepared in Coaching Session 43) into a format that can be used by anybody within the business.

You may have heard of an 'operations manual', which is simply a document that details all of the systems within a business. Although this may seem like overkill for a startup, an operations manual allows you to test the processes and refine them as necessary. The necessity of an operations manual varies from business to business, as a startup that intends to stay small (say one or two staff) would almost certainly not require a full manual.

A well-prepared operations manual can provide several benefits to the business owner. It allows staff to be trained more effectively, and in theory should reduce the risk of system failures in the business provided that the manual is actually used. More importantly, it gives the business a platform for growth, as the systems can be designed in a way that can be replicated within other locations.

Finally, there is the added benefit of the increase in value of the business! Although there is a huge time commitment in building systems and manuals, any eventual buyer of the business is effectively buying these systems, and as such the value of the business will increase based on the level of systemization within the business.

FINDING THE RIGHT PEOPLE TO WORK WITHIN THESE SYSTEMS

In the previous chapter we looked conceptually at how an organization chart is put together and how the recruitment process should proceed. One of the vital elements of the recruitment process is a strong job description, which sets out exactly what is required from the staff member in a particular role. It should include the functions in which the staff member will be expected to work, and the specific processes that they will be responsible for.

Job descriptions are normally structured as a combination of a list of competencies and some narrative, and must be free of any potential discrimination so that you ensure that you stay on the right side of the law.

An effective job description will not only form part of your future operations manual, but should also act as part of the marketing collateral for the role.

An example job description would be as follows:

Job Description – Accounts Assistant

GENERAL DESCRIPTION

This role is for an accounts assistant to assist the Finance Controller and Finance Director with the upkeep of the company's financial records, and to ensure that the company adheres to its statutory and commercial obligations.

PRIMARY JOB FUNCTIONS

- Recording income for the business
- Reconciling income to cash receipts in the till every evening
- Reporting on potential bad debts
- Reporting on outstanding debtors
- Credit control
- Paying suppliers by cheque
- Recording petty cash transactions
- Reporting on outstanding creditors
- Processing transactions on an accounting system
- Reconciling the bank accounts to ensure completeness
- Processing accounting adjustments (such as depreciation)

REQUIRED SKILLS

- Strong analytical skills
- Strong IT skills, particularly in Microsoft Office and Windows
- Attention to detail
- Strong written and verbal communication skills
- Ability to handle customers and suppliers professionally at all times

DESIRED SKILLS AND EXPERIENCE

- Experience in a credit control function
- Experience with Quickbooks accounting software
- Managerial experience
- Full driving licence

EDUCATION

AAT Qualified, or qualified by experience

WORK STATUS

Full time, reporting to Finance Controller

HOW SHOULD A BUSINESS GROW?

Should business growth be an intention of yours, there are a number of routes for business expansion open to you. Each of these has certain advantages and disadvantages. Some methods of growth include:

Organic growth

Most businesses tend towards organic growth, based on their marketing efforts and referrals from their existing customers. Together with inflation, this leads to organic growth provided that the number of new customers exceeds the number of customers that stop using the business.

It is very difficult to achieve rapid organic growth, unless you have a strong funding base and a clearly defined differentiator to set yourself apart in the market. The key to organic growth is to ensure that you have realistic ambitions given the capital available in the business, and also to make sure that you don't over spend in pursuit of aggressive growth.

Funded growth

Some businesses, particularly in the technology sector, look towards angel investors and venture capital investors to provide funding for accelerated growth. Whilst this resolves the funding base requirement of rapid organic growth, the investors will be looking for a very strong business, and a plan that allows them to execute an exit plan with a reasonable chance of success.

Franchising

Business format franchising is a route of expansion for businesses which either do not have the funding or the appetite for organic or funded growth. It has a strong benefit in that the franchisee is motivated to make his or her own business a success, far more than an employed manager may be. On the flip side, the ownership of the entirety of the business is distributed, which might not suit the desired end result of the prospective franchisor. Sometimes, companies that are company owned (and developed organically) in their home territory are franchised overseas, so that the business can benefit from the input of a master franchise owner who understands the local customs and market. Examples of franchises include McDonald's, Dominos Pizza and Subway.

Licensing

As there is no legal definition of franchising or licensing, the split between the two can seem to be a grey area. Broadly speaking, a business format franchise offers the franchisee access to the brand and systems of the franchisor, and with that comes a level of obligation and control that is set out in the franchise agreement. A licence is usually structured as a more 'hands off' agreement than a franchise, with less control and usually less management assistance from the franchisor. Licensing is often used for software products, and also for distribution of brands such as Coca-Cola.

Mergers and acquisitions

Strategic mergers and acquisitions are another route for businesses to achieve growth. Especially prevalent in the professional sectors, an acquisition allows a business to scale rapidly without the delays that organic growth, funded growth or franchising can cause. From a logical perspective, before considering an acquisition you should consider the following:

- Is there a *synergy* with your existing business – will 2 + 2 = 5 as a result of the merger/acquisition?
- Will the merger/acquisition take focus away from your core business?
- Do the cultures of the two businesses match, or will there be some management issues ahead?
- Do the businesses have similar customers, or are there differences that will need to be managed?
- Will the merger/acquisition cost more than simply marketing and growing organically?
- Are there any non-financial reasons for the merger/acquisition?

COACHING SESSION 45

Growth

What methods of growth appear attractive to you? What would work for your business, and what wouldn't? Will this help you achieve your goals set out at the start of the book? Note your initial thoughts below:

Growth (*cont.*)

There is no right way to grow a business, as every business has its own unique factors to consider. In addition to this, certain methods of growth are ideal for some sectors but not for others – for example, business format franchising works very well for retailers and consumer service businesses, but is a bit more difficult for professional service organizations due to the levels of training required.

Regardless of the route that you choose for growing your business, if of course growth is a desire of yours, you should take professional impartial advice to make sure that the route that you consider is appropriate for you and your business, and to understand the financial and business implications of the growth.

One thing that is important to always bear in mind is that the nature of your role as a business owner will change as the business grows. As your team grows, so will the role expected from you. You will find that whereas in the early days you had a personal relationship with every staff member, this will later be taken on by the management team and you will be more detached from the day-to-day operations of the business.

→ NEXT STEPS

In this chapter, we have looked at the difference between business functions and business processes, and then explored how to set up a system for these processes. We've performed this work for an example function and process, and next you will need to perform this for other areas of the business. Perhaps more importantly, we've looked at the difference between the person and the position. It is always important to remember in the early days that you will often require an individual to perform more than one job on the organization chart.

We have also explored the various ways that businesses can grow, both organically and more aggressively. These methods include business format franchising, licensing, and mergers. Each of these could justify a book in their own right, and are worth considering in the early days so that you can build your business with the correct intentions. In any event, a business will undoubtedly benefit from a well-prepared operations manual. Even if you don't decide to franchise or license your brand, it will add value to the business and will hopefully serve you well by increasing profit and your eventual sale price, should you decide to exit.

I've included notes of some great resources in the 'further reading' section which can develop your understanding of business further, should you wish to explore the potential future growth of your business.

FURTHER READING

Useful resources

Gerber, Michael E,, *The E-Myth Revisited*, HarperBusiness, 2001

Sawyer, Clive, *How to Franchise Your Business: The Plain Speaking Guide*, Live It, 2011

Duckett, Brian, *How to Franchise your Business*, How To Books, 2011

Duncan, Lee, *How to Double your Business*, Financial Times/Prentice Hall, 2012

TAKEAWAYS

What is my action plan for systemizing the business?

What next steps do I need to take, and when will I achieve these by? Do I need any help along the way?

10 PROMOTING YOUR BUSINESS

- How to bring customers into your business
- How to monitor your marketing and advertising spend
- What to expect when marketing your business

This chapter has been deliberately left towards the end of the book, as I've seen too many businesses that are great at promoting themselves but not too good at running the business behind the scenes. Now that we have structured the business appropriately, and have the administration systems in place, it's time to look at how a startup business can promote itself to its potential customers.

Promoting your business uses all of the knowledge that you have obtained along this journey, as you need to have a clear vision of who you are, how you are different and why a customer would buy from you. What's more, it doesn't need to be expensive, however it does require attention and repeated action to ensure that the customers keep coming in.

There is an often heard quote: 'Half of my marketing works, the problem is I don't know which half'. Even with the very best marketing experts and reporting systems, you will never know categorically which marketing campaigns are effective and which aren't. This is because a customer often requires several 'touch points' to buy from you. For example, a customer might see a billboard advert, but not take action. The next week they might see an advert in the newspaper, which reinforces your brand. Three months later, they might have seen a leaflet in the rack at a local shop, and also they might have seen you and heard about your business from both you and other customers at local networking events. However, they end up purchasing from you by searching for your company name and clicking on a paid search engine link.

Regardless of the final method that they used to purchase from you, there has clearly been a process of awareness building which supported the final purchasing stage, as it is unlikely that they would have searched for your company name without the prior awareness building. This is where the power of branding and repeated action comes into play.

BUILDING AN EFFECTIVE BRAND FOR A STARTUP

Although a marketer at heart, and having a passion for the development of brands, I am a strong believer that the brand has to be fit for purpose for the business to which it relates. You've no doubt heard about the extraordinary amounts that some branding agencies charge, and quite frankly it is irrelevant for all but certain types of business. There is however a strong reason to gauge the right level of branding and design support for your business.

You need to consider how essential a strong brand is to your business. The promotion of an internet business is dependent on its brand name and domain – it needs to be catchy and memorable. However, if your intention is to be a small local business, then a flashy logo and website might well be wasted money.

Having said the above, unless you are a graphic designer by trade I would strongly recommend enlisting the help of a designer to produce your marketing material, as it will help you have a professional image to the outside world. Logos can range from £50 to £50,000, so there's not always the need to spend huge amounts of money to have a logo professionally designed. In fact, the strongest brand image that I have put together myself cost me £300 including a full brand guideline document and a pre-designed template for all stationery and corporate communications. Make sure that you see copies of the designer's work before proceeding, and also that you have the ability to make revisions to their proposals.

Domain names are another item that can benefit from a branding mindset. A good domain name is simple, has no hyphens or other characters, and is short enough to read out over the telephone. Personally I try to stick to either .com or .co.uk domains, however there are a number of other domain endings available now, and my understanding of current thinking is that eventually these endings will become irrelevant.

◖◗ COACHING SESSION 46

Branding

Now the fun begins – brainstorming a name and brand vision for your business!

Think of the image you would like to project for your business – what are the buzzwords (e.g. honesty, efficiency, premier, innovative):

Brand vision *(cont.)*

Now think of some names that would be consistent with the above:

Finally, list some available domain names (using a domain name checker online):

Having done the above Coaching Session, use this as a template to brief your designer about logos and colour schemes. As with all suppliers, you should use their experience and value their opinions, however please also make sure that you follow your gut feeling if something isn't right.

COACHING SESSION 47

Costs

It's important to ensure that your brand is sufficiently developed, however this shouldn't be at huge cost in relation to the type of business, nor in relation to direct marketing that can be directly correlated to new business. Of your total marketing budget (refer back to your financial projections), how much do you believe should be allocated to branding, and how should it be allocated?

	£
Logo design	_____
Stationery design	_____
Website design	_____
Website build	_____
Other (list below):	£
_____	_____
_____	_____
_____	_____
_____	_____
Total	_____

BRAND PROTECTION

Once you have a logo, you then need to consider how you would protect it. Trademarking a logo isn't essential, and I would wager that most businesses don't even bother. It does however add some value to the imagery (and potentially words) that you have come up with, and it is something that would become vital as you look to grow.

Registering a trademark is relatively simple, and you can either do it yourself through the IPO (Intellectual Property Office), or through a trademark attorney. Typically a trademark would cost you approximately £200 if registered yourself, or £500–£600 if you engage a professional to do it. There are different fees based on how many classes (types of business) you would like to register the mark for, and the whole process takes some time as the IPO has to check that there are no competing marks, and also that the registration is publicized should there be any objections.

Provided that the trademark fulfils the criteria set by the IPO – in that it is distinctive, that it's not descriptive, not offensive, not deceptive, and not customary for your industry, the process should be relatively pain free. If however there is a dispute over the eligibility of a mark, it is worth seeking professional advice and weighing up whether it is worth proceeding with registration. I've personally registered marks myself and via professionals, and the attorneys know how to present a case in the event of a dispute, which I would not have otherwise been able to put forwards.

You would also need to consider whether you wish to register just a logo or words, and also whether you would like to register for just the UK or also overseas.

MARKETING THEORY

There are a range of marketing theories, and indeed much like accountancy and other skills included in this guide, there are extensive qualifications available, and as such it is impossible to provide full details of marketing theory, which would be several books in its own right! I would however highlight a few key theories which are always worth bearing in mind when constructing any promotional campaign:

- **Push versus pull marketing**. I'm a great believer in producing marketing which attracts the buyer to want to know more and engage with you in conversation, rather than traditional 'disruptive' marketing which blasts promotional messages at the buyer.

- **AIDA**. Attention Interest Desire Action is a historic model which shows the steps that a buyer takes before deciding to buy. At each stage of this process a percentage of your buyers drop out, and it's important to attempt to tick each box when targeting a market.

- **Product positioning**. Popularized by Michael Porter, it is vital to understand your product positioning, and whether you will be a high volume, low cost business; or conversely a low volume, high value business.

- **Features versus benefits**. Whenever you create a marketing message it is vital to focus on the benefits of the product or service, rather than the features.

- **Multiple touch points**. As referred to earlier, often a customer needs to hear about you several times before deciding to buy.

- **Split testing**. One of the best ways of defining your marketing message and optimizing your results is by 'split testing' – in other words, trying two versions of an advert / website, and seeing which performs better. Even the big brands such as McDonald's still do this to continually refine their marketing efforts.

- **Web user behaviour**. It is always important to understand how the typical web user behaves on a website. For example, this will help you understand where to place your logo, and any call to action. Heat maps can help you with this.

PROMOTING YOUR BUSINESS ONLINE

Now we'll look at how to promote your business, and we'll start with online promotion, as it can be the most cost-effective method of marketing if done correctly.

The first question you need to ask yourself is whether you need a website. For all but the very smallest businesses, I would strongly suggest yes, as this is your online brochure that almost everybody who comes into contact with you would check before doing business with you.

> **! COACH'S TIP**
>
> A good website doesn't need to be expensive, nor filled with content. It simply needs to be well designed (ideally not a template), up to date, and provide the visitor with a 'call to action' (the next steps to take them from being a visitor to engaging with you).

Landing pages and email marketing

Some of the best websites have separately designed landing pages, which are effectively sales letters created for a specific marketing campaign. These will then offer some free information (for example an e-book or a video) in return for the prospect's details. This then provides the business with a lead that can be contacted regularly, and a proportion of these will end up becoming paying customers provided that contact is maintained.

Email marketing is a highly effective way of communicating with prospects, and unlike traditional direct mail it comes at virtually no cost. There is however a fine balance that needs to be considered, as an email campaign can very quickly be considered 'spam' if it annoys the prospect, is too frequent, or is not requested. You must make sure that you stick to the law surrounding such communications, and offer readers the opportunity to unsubscribe. A safe way of performing email marketing is to use a third party software application such as MailChimp or AWeber, which would also give you analytics information on how your campaigns are performing.

Any form of marketing fundamentally comes down to conversion rates, and in an email marketing campaign the three rates you need to monitor are the open rates, the click through rates, and the unsubscribe rates. The open rates can be optimized through choosing effective titles for your emails, which grab the reader's attention. Providing teaser content, with further content available on the subsequent landing page, often increases click through rates. Finally, unsubscribe rates are ultimately managed by ensuring that your emails provide valuable content for your readers.

COACHING SESSION 48

Landing page

Landing pages are a highly effective way of ensuring that your website visitors get directed to a targeted sales page, and hence these tend to improve conversion rates from these visitors. Think about potential landing pages for your site. Do you have key services that would benefit from their own page? Perhaps you have unique products, or specialisms in a certain market? Consider the search terms that your customers might use to find you through a search engine, and then in turn landing pages that can be generated to capture these visitors:

Landing page (*cont.*)

Social media

The latest buzz in marketing circles is around social media, and you may have had some experience of using some of the following platforms:

- **Facebook**. The most well-known social media platform, allowing visitors to connect with friends and family, and share a variety of media.

- **YouTube**. A video sharing site, with comment and subscribing functionality.

- **Twitter**. A 'micro-blogging' site which allows users to share updates of 140 characters or less.

- **Instagram**. A photo-sharing site, similar to Twitter but for images rather than text.

- **LinkedIn**. A corporate social media site, hosting a 'directory' of individuals and corporates in business.

There are many other applications, such as Snapchat, Pinterest, Vine, Google Plus and Tumblr. Each platform has its own community, and the content that may be appropriate for LinkedIn may not be for Facebook, and vice versa. Social media marketing is fast becoming a field of its own, with various experts promoting their services to help your business take advantage of these platforms. Whilst these services are undoubtedly of benefit for some businesses, my advice is to become an observer of those networks you don't know about, so that you can learn the culture of each network.

It's also important to keep up to date with the changes on each platform. For example, on Twitter it was commonplace to receive an automated message (DM) every time you followed a new business. Nowadays, this practice is frowned upon. Many platforms have also moved towards paid advertising, which allows you to either sponsor posts or place adverts in your contacts news feeds. The targeting available through these platforms, using the information entered by the users themselves, is very specific and can be used with great impact.

COACH'S TIP

A question that I'm commonly asked at workshops is whether a business owner should post on social media sites as themselves or as a business. Personally, I've adopted the view that people engage with people, and as such I have an active personal profile alongside my business profiles. Many brands have successfully introduced personality into their corporate feeds, with Tesco's and Sainsbury's being two examples of companies that have a human feel to their Twitter feeds.

Another common question I am asked surrounds the volume of posts, and the types of posts. Each platform has a different level of acceptability in terms of post volume. For example, Twitter tends to be rather fast paced, and to be visible it is best to post several times per day. Conversely, the news feed on LinkedIn is far slower and this volume of posting would be frowned upon. Broadly speaking, I look towards a simple rule of thirds when it comes to posting – one third being my own original content / updates, one third being replies and interaction, and one third being the sharing of other material that I believe my followers would appreciate.

COACHING SESSION 49

Social media

From the above descriptions, and any knowledge you already have of social networking, which social networks do you believe would be most beneficial for your business?

Which social networks do you feel that you need to devote some time to, so that you can learn more about how they work and how best to promote your business? List an action plan for you to learn more about these networks:

Making social media manageable

There are a number of tools out there that help business owners (and indeed individuals) manage their social media presence.

One of my favourite tools is an application called Buffer (https://bufferapp. com). It allows you to store a 'buffer' of social media posts, to be released during the day at pre-determined times. This tool also allows you to store 'retweets' on Twitter, meaning that you can devote a concentrated block of time to social media and then let the system drip feed these posts for you.

Another great tool is Hootsuite. This allows you to manage various social media accounts, and will allow you to schedule a number of updates which can be imported from a simple spreadsheet. What's more, the software allows you to connect to link shorteners such as https://bitly.com so that you can have your own custom domain (think branding!) and also you can monitor the performance of your updates.

Search engine optimization and search engine marketing

Once you have your website and social media platforms set up, you will still need to attract visitors to your sites. Historically, there were a number of techniques that you could use to improve your 'ranking' (position) on Google, the leading search engine. Such methods included link building, keyword inclusion, domain name management, meta tag development, and various other tricks.

The search engines have become wise to this, as there was a whole industry devoted to building sites to get to the top of a specific search term. Obviously, this goes against Google's aim of being a valuable search function for its end user, and it would prefer for a site with relevant content to be listed above a site that has merely paid someone to manipulate the results.

Nowadays, search engine optimization is less effective than before, not least because Google changes their algorithms regularly, which can significantly affect a website's position online. My suggestion therefore is to recruit a web development team who are up to date with what is happening with regards search engine visibility, but do not become a slave to it!

Search engines such as Google and Bing also offer sponsored links at the top of their results. These are offered on a 'cost per click' basis, meaning that in theory you only pay for results. The cost is calculated on an auction basis, with the highest bidder paying for the prime positions. I say in theory because, in fact, you do not generate any business from a click through to your website – instead you only generate business from the subsequent conversions. Again, as with email marketing, you need to monitor your click through rates and your conversion rates on the landing page. It is also worth monitoring your 'quality score', which is a score that the search engine will give you regarding the relevance of your site compared to the advert. This will impact on your ultimate cost per click, and it will depend partly on both your conversion rates on the search page (in other words, what percentage of 'impressions' result in a click), and the bounce rate (early exit rate) of your site.

> ## COACH'S TIP
>
> As with social media, there are a number of companies that will offer to manage your pay per click campaigns for you. I believe that this is often a wise investment in theory, as the companies have invested themselves in bespoke bid management software and the knowledge needed to generate lots of cheap clicks. I would just say that you need to consider the management cost divided over the total number of clicks, to give you an effective click cost, as if you have a low search keyword this can increase the cost to you significantly.

Finally, bear in mind that the majority of the work performed by these agencies is in the first month or so, as they build and develop your campaigns and keywords. Once this has been done, you might find that you can manage the ongoing bidding and account settings yourself.

OFFLINE MARKETING

Much is written about online marketing, however unless you have an unlimited budget for search engine advertisements, you will still want to attract customers to your website or social media platforms through traditional marketing methods. An interesting development in offline marketing is that businesses now tend to direct customers to a specific email address or website, rather than to a phone number.

Some of the more popular methods of offline marketing are as follows:

- **Direct mail.** In the online world, direct mail shots are becoming a rarity due to their cost, and as such the success rates have increased now that there is little competition in the mail!

- **Telemarketing.** Calling prospects to open the conversation is a good way to start a business relationship if you can add value within the first few sentences; however you must be aware of the Telephone Preference Service (http://www.tpsonline.org.uk).

- **Networking.** Meeting people face to face is a great way of building relationships, which in turn can lead to them (or their contacts) becoming prospective customers. Make sure that you don't commit the cardinal sin of selling *at* people!

- **Leaflet drops.** Posting leaflets through people's doors can work, but be careful about who you choose to do it – some agencies deliver batches of leaflets, meaning that your message is often discarded with ten other leaflets. Try something innovative, maybe a post-it note on the letterbox?

- **Advertisements.** Adverts in local press and magazines are a great brand builder, provided that you are in a position to risk paying money solely for brand building.

- **Referrals.** Customer referrals are the best possible form of marketing, as your customer will actively sell your service, leaving you to simply take the order! To generate referrals, you will need a systemized approach, and of course you will need to truly provide great service to all of your customers.

COACHING SESSION 50

Offline marketing

The above list of offline marketing activities is in no way exhaustive. Using the above, together with your experiences as a customer, prepare a list of potential ways that you can promote your business offline:

One of the biggest disadvantages of offline marketing when compared to online marketing is the lack of detailed statistics behind activities. With most online activities, you pay on results, or can at least monitor the performance of every single advert. With offline advertising, you must be diligent in asking the customer how they heard of you so that you can track the performance of each and every activity – but also bear in mind the impact of multiple touch points (as described earlier), which won't be in the customer's mind when they find you.

HOW TO CREATE A MARKETING PLAN

To effectively market your business, it is important that your marketing activities are planned, recorded and monitored. There is little point spending on marketing for the sake of marketing – instead, each activity should have a clearly defined outcome. Not all activities can be correlated directly to new business, however the purpose of each marketing activity should be weighed up, so that you can compare the costs (and return) of each different form of marketing.

As a rule of thumb, my belief is that unless you are heavily reliant on a brand image (for example, a website might be extremely reliant on a catchy domain name), you should only spend 30 per cent of your first year marketing budget on branding, reducing to a maximum of 10 per cent thereafter. This 10 per cent should mostly be put into 'reserve', saved for a refresh of branding every three to five years.

The remainder of your activities can be mapped out on a marketing plan, with expected spend and also expected return set out for each activity. The most powerful part of this process comes when you then record the actual spend and return on each activity, as this gives you the ability to monitor your spend and calculate a cost per lead for each activity.

When preparing a marketing plan, it is always worth considering whether there are any seasonal trends that you should capitalize on. A fashion retail store would typically focus on clothing seasons, and the sale periods at the end of these. Likewise, a coffee shop might focus on seasonal promotions, selling mince pies at Christmas and iced drinks in the summer.

COACHING SESSION 51

Seasonal trends

For each month, consider a marketing message that your business could convey. It may be that you focus on bank holidays, celebrations such as Valentine's Day, or religious events. Think both about how you could attract customers during this time, and also any seasonal offers that you could provide:

January

February

March

April

May

June

July

August

September

October

November

December

→ NEXT STEPS

In this chapter, we have looked at a wide range of marketing activities that you can implement within your business. We've looked at the importance of promotion, and making sure that you have a variety of touch points with your customers. We've also considered the difference between brand building and direct marketing, and looked at different types of online and offline marketing.

We've also explored marketing ideas specific to your business, and begun the development of a marketing plan, with seasonal promotions and offers.

Finally, we touched on some of the theoretical aspects of marketing. This is an area that fascinates me personally, so I've included some suggested reading within the 'Further Reading' section.

ONLINE RESOURCE

This can be further developed using the template available at www.TYCoachbook.com/Startup

FURTHER READING

Useful resources:

Blick, Dee, *The Ultimate Small Business Marketing Book*, Filament Publishing, 2011

Blick, Dee, *The 15 Essential Marketing Masterclasses for your Small Business*, [publisher year]

Kriel, Nicky, *How to Twitter for Business Success*, The Other Publishing Company, 2013

Carvill, Michelle, *The Business of Being Social*, Crimson Publishing, 2013

Thomas, Bryony, *Watertight Marketing*, Ecademy Press Limited, 2013

TAKEAWAYS

What areas of marketing do I need to develop my understanding in?

How will I go about promoting my business?

What are my next action points?

11 KEEPING SANE IN BUSINESS

✔ IN THIS CHAPTER YOU WILL LEARN

- How to maintain an effective work–life balance
- The art of time management
- How to make sure that your business is exactly what you want

We've now covered a range of topics, from the basics of evaluating an idea through to some of the considerations of day-to-day trading. It's time now to take a step back from the detail, and re-consider why you are going into business, so that you can ensure that you don't fall into the traps that I see so many business owners fall into. During this, we'll refocus on some areas previously covered to make sure that attention is paid to these, in an attempt to minimize the risk of these issues becoming a problem for you.

Without doubt, a business benefits from its owner being fresh and enthusiastic about it. The boost that a motivated entrepreneur can bring to a business is phenomenal, and conversely a tired, demotivated business owner can end up dragging the business down without realizing. So, it is vital that we explore some of the common problems that business owners suffer from:

- **Becoming a bottleneck**. If I was to choose just one issue that limits both businesses and entrepreneurs, it is this. Often a business owner will want to become involved in every little detail of the business. Whilst it is important to understand the workings of the business, it's also important to remember that there are only 24 hours in each day, and by becoming personally involved in every single process, the business is limited by the time and effort that you can put into it.

- **Not having sufficient separation between personal and business life**. A quote that I have heard is that *the best part of being an entrepreneur is that you can choose which 18 hours per day that you work!* The very nature of running a startup means that you have to cut costs wherever possible, and this often means that you will be working from the dining room table. Add to that the pressures of starting a business – with a lack of staff, and the additional promotional efforts needed – and you have the perfect recipe for long days (and nights) slaving away at a business.

- **Irregular income.** It is understandable that the biggest fear that most people have about starting their own business is the lack of a secure pay cheque, and to many business owners the shift from a regular monthly income to perhaps an irregular income (or worse still, no income) is a very difficult change to make. This is compounded by the additional pressures that running a startup can put on an entrepreneur (see above).

- **Working outside the skill set of the entrepreneur.** Although a business owner may be highly skilled in what they do (whether that's a technical skill, a sales skill, or a management skill), they may not necessarily have the other skills required to run a business. These include areas such as negotiation, decision making, leadership, in addition to those skills more commonly seen in employees. Often, these skills can't be learned from a book or a seminar, and as such the business owner has to learn by experience. Along the way some mistakes will be made, and the stress that can occur from these is yet another pressure for the entrepreneur.

COACHING SESSION 52

Troubleshooting

We've covered some typical problems that business owners can encounter, which can cause work-related stress and ultimately affect their performance. Needless to say this can also have a knock-on effect to the performance of the startup. Can you think of any more potential problems that can arise? Use some examples from your personal experiences so far, as often the same stresses that affect an employed individual can affect a business owner:

Troubleshooting (*cont.*)

In his book *The 4-Hour Workweek*, Tim Ferriss explores some of the aforementioned problems, and explains how he had experienced them himself. He then looks at a number of strategies, ranging from simple auto response systems and the use of personal assistants, through to some more radical solutions, to help individuals overcome these issues.

I mentioned earlier that becoming a bottleneck is the biggest issue for entrepreneurs and their businesses. If properly performed, the systems development that we discussed in Chapter 9 should help remove the risk of this happening. By having formal systems, you remove the theoretical need to be involved in every detail of the business. Whilst this might work on paper, the reality is that the business owner has to also make an emotional change and be able to let go of the details, for the good of the business.

Finding an adequate balance between your working life and personal life is also paramount to your success as a business owner. Although the business might currently be at the forefront of your life at this stage, it's essential that you also make time for family, friends, and anything else that is important to you. It is unfortunately too tempting for a 'nine to five' to become a 'six to midnight' if you work from home, and ultimately this will be a recipe for poor health and poor relationships.

COACHINGSESSION 53

Work–life balance

Take some time now to make some commitments to yourself. Think about activities that you can do, or routines that you can put in place, to make sure that your business doesn't succeed to the detriment of your personal life. It may be that you decide to allocate a certain day as a 'family day'. You might decide to visit the gym three times a week. Try to focus on the following areas:

Relationships

Leisure

Family and friends

Health

Other (spirituality/creativity etc.)

By making the above commitments, you can try to prevent the issues that can arise from a lack of separation between working life and personal life. Although it may seem like you are sacrificing some valuable time that could be put into the business, it will help you be a happy and healthy business owner in the long term.

THE ART OF TIME MANAGEMENT

As with most topics covered in this book, time management could be (and indeed is) a subject in its own right, and there are various books available, some of which have been detailed at the end of the chapter.

In his book *The 7 Habits of Highly Effective People*, the author (Stephen R. Covey) discusses his model of time allocation. Often, people fail to differentiate between what is important and what is urgent. As an example, you may rush to answer a ringing phone, but not devote the time to strategic planning. There is no indication of whether the ringing phone is important, yet there is certainly an urgency as it will otherwise divert to voicemail. Whereas with the strategic planning, there is no urgency and it's quite possible to carry on through your whole life without it – however the future will suffer if this doesn't take place.

- **Important and Urgent.** These are tasks that are both important in the end vision for the business, but also require a timely action. These are often dealt with as priorities, and rightly so.

- **Not Important and Urgent.** Covey contends that most 'urgent' issues that people fill their days with are within this quadrant. They can either be dealt with by someone else, or are perhaps not aligned to your end goals. These are the matters that can be resolved by building effective systems and consciously choosing where to allocate your time.

- **Important and Not Urgent.** These are the tasks that really matter. Included within this heading would be goal-setting, strategic planning, and systems development. Ultimately, these are the tasks that should be prioritized over the 'not important and urgent', as the completion of these should lead to a reduction in unimportant tasks. Because there are no deadlines that come with these tasks, it's important that you set your own deadlines to ensure that they actually happen.

- **Not Important and Not Urgent.** This is the last of Covey's time allocations, and anything that is in this quadrant should be questioned – if it is not urgent, and it is not important, why are you doing it?

COACHING SESSION 54

Time management

Complete the following time management quadrant, using your current 'to-do' list, with some examples of each type of task. This will help prepare you for allocating future tasks as a business owner:

Important and Not Urgent	*Important and Urgent*
Not Important and Urgent	*Not Important and Not Urgent*

The next factor that can cause stress in entrepreneurs is the irregularity of personal drawings from the business. As an employee, you should be able to rely on your employer paying you a fixed wage each and every month until you leave the company, provided that the company doesn't go into liquidation. When you run your own business, you don't have that luxury. To help you plan for this, you can take the following steps:

1. **Establish your monthly living expenses.** As simple as it sounds, the first step is to work out what you need to live on, month by month. This will then be your intended monthly draw from the business. Make sure you take into account a contingency for unexpected expenses, and a provision for any personal tax liabilities.

2. **Make sure your monthly draw is in your projections.** If you have under-estimated this amount, make sure that you revise your projections accordingly. Realistically, your bank manager will expect you to make a reasonable drawing each month for your living expenses, and so there is no problem with this being included. They might question the amount if it is felt to be excessive!

3. **Stick to the monthly drawings.** Try to avoid the temptation of withdrawing more than you need if you have a good month. Although there is always a temptation to reward yourself, remember that business income is often cyclical and a good month may be followed by a few poor months!

ΩΩ COACHING SESSION 55

Review

Now it's time to revisit some previous exercises to make sure that you have projected your monthly expenses correctly! Firstly, revisit Coaching Session 1 in Chapter 1. Is this projection still appropriate? Are there any changes you can make which weren't identified earlier? Have your circumstances changed at all?

Next, revisit your financial projections that make up part of your business plan. Have you reflected the correct monthly income in your projections? Is there a sufficient reserve of capital to cover months where the profit of the business isn't enough to pay your drawings?

Note below any required changes:

The final problem identified earlier in this chapter was the need for entrepreneurs to work outside of their natural skill set. You might recall that during Coaching Session 5 in Chapter 1, we reviewed some typical skills of an entrepreneur at a high level. Although development needs were noted at this point, it is likely that you would have found more gaps in your knowledge and experience whilst working through the book.

There are a number of ways that you can develop skills in business:

- **Seminars**. Many companies will offer you training seminars which can help you understand topics such as sales, marketing, finance and leadership. In my opinion, one of the main benefits of attending a seminar is the networking opportunities which arise from meeting the other attendees. On the flip side, the content is often very generic and may not necessarily be relevant for your business.

- **College courses**. Many adult education centres offer part-time courses which might be of value; however the content is often theoretical and intended to be studied by somebody who is looking to become an expert in that particular area, rather than business owners who require a rounded skill set.

- **Books**. There are some great books out there which cover a variety of areas, and I've included some of the best that I've found in the further reading section of this book. Financially, a book is often the most cost-effective way of gaining the information when compared to seminars and formal education, although one of the main problems with books is that you can't ask questions to explore certain areas further.

- **Online courses**. Nowadays there is a wealth of information available online, including videos and blogs. Business forums may also be a great way for you to gain feedback and advice from peers who would have been through the same learning curve that you have.

COACHING SESSION 56

Further development

It's time to revisit previous work again! Review Coaching Session 5 from Chapter 1, and note below any further development required. This may include more specific areas, as the previous Coaching Session was intended to be completed at a high level.

COACHING SESSION 57

Prioritize

Coaching Session 5 and Coaching Session 56 should now give you, a comprehensive list of development requirements, so it is time to prioritize your development needs and investigate the options available for development in the top five areas. Make notes and commit to actions on each of these areas below:

Development Area 1:

Development Area 2:

Development Area 3:

Development Area 4:

Development Area 5:

Having addressed the specific problems that I hear from business owners, there is often an unspoken problem, which is much harder to define. Sometimes, people start a business to move away from a specific problem – they either want to feel in control of what they do, remove any earnings limits that they might have in employment, or they wish to choose the hours that they work. Unfortunately, a business can consume them far more than a job ever could. This leads to an uncomfortable position where the business actually becomes a far bigger problem than their job ever was, and they wonder whether the grass really was greener on the other side.

I believe that this feeling comes about from the simple fact that the demands of being in business often conflict with the business owners' paradigms about how they should live.

COACHING SESSION 58

Why do you want to start up a business?

In Coaching Session 3 of Chapter 1, we explored the reasons why you were looking at starting in business. Now, please note below any fears that you may have about being in business, given the above narrative, and actions that you will take to prevent these issues from occurring:

It's paramount that you take steps to ensure that these issues don't arise, as prevention is always far easier than the cure. Simple steps, such as the commitments that you made in Coaching Session 53 of this chapter, will help you make sure that you stay on the right path with regards your personal life.

You should also make sure that you stay on the right path for your overall goals. In Chapters 1 and 2, we discussed the importance of goal-setting, and within the Coaching Sessions we set some goals for you personally and for your business.

> ## ! COACH'S TIP
>
> I cannot stress enough that one of the vital elements of goal-setting is a continual review and refinement of your goals. I can say this from personal experience – you might remember in Chapter 1 I referred to the 'empty' feeling that I had when I'd completed my goals that were set years before. This feeling was all due to the lack of direction that I felt once the goals were achieved. Obviously I was happy to have bought a Range Rover Sport, and to have met the other targets that I'd set myself, but the lack of anything further to aim for was unknowingly limiting me at that time.

WHERE TO GET SUPPORT WHEN YOU ARE IN BUSINESS?

Although much of this book has been positive and forward looking, the reality is that being in business brings ups and downs to your life, much in the same way that you'd experience being employed. The difference is that as an employee, many other people have shared your experiences and feel able to offer support, whereas as a startup owner it is far more difficult to have support from those who have trodden the same path as you.

There is also the very fine balance of the image that you want to project to the outside world. If you are uncertain about a specific feature of your product, or not too sure that your customer service is hitting the mark, then the last thing you want to do is confide in somebody who may be a potential customer or referrer for your business.

Many people look to online business forums and social media for support – an example being the UK Business Forums. These internet forums allow you to post updates confidentially, which can help you receive feedback that isn't linked back to your business.

If you have appointed an informal advisory board, as suggested in Chapter 3, they can also provide you with assistance, and due to the lack of anonymity you can be sure of their qualification to advise you. Business coaches and mentors can also offer much the same role, but bear in mind that you will likely have to pay for this support.

Finally, although it might seem obvious, be sure to involve your partner/spouse where possible! Although they might not have had experience in business themselves, a clear understanding of the issues that you are going through will help them to support you during what can be a difficult time for many.

→ NEXT STEPS

In this chapter you have pulled together a clearer picture of your own personal position before starting a business. The Coaching Sessions have allowed you to appraise both your financial position, and also your motivations for starting a business. By setting these out on paper, you can weigh up the pros and cons of moving forwards, as if you are not fully prepared for starting a business, it can have a devastating impact on your family life and your finances.

You have also been able to evaluate your experiences to date. You have probably seen that although a previous job may have focused on a specific role, the skills that are required by entrepreneurs are often used within these roles too. For example, a checkout assistant at a supermarket would be expected to provide customer service, financial accountability, relationship building and quite possibly sales skills!

This process of self-evaluation will allow you to identify any areas that you need to work on before proceeding with the business idea, before you get too far into this process. Our next step is to evaluate the business itself, in much the same way that we have evaluated you personally as a business owner.

FURTHER READING

Gerber, Michael E., *The E-Myth Revisited*, (HarperBusiness, 2001)

Kiyosaki, Robert, *Rich Dad, Poor Dad*, (Plata Publishing, 2011)

Kiyosaki, Robert, *Rich Dad, Poor Dad 2: The Cashflow Quadrant*, (Plata Publishing, 2011)

Covey, Stephen R., *The 7 Habits of Highly Effective People*, (Simon & Schuster, 2004)

Ferriss, Tim, *The 4-Hour Workweek*, (Vermillion, 2011)

TAKEAWAYS

What are the warning signs that I need to look out for?

Are there any areas that I can address now, to prevent future problems?

What actions do I need to take going forwards?t

ACTION PLAN

It's now time to think about your goals you are going to take on having read the book, and dig a little deeper into what you thought about it:

What were the **five** main things that surprised you about the book and why?

-
-
-
-
-

What will you keep doing, do more of and do less? Please fill in the table below:

	Tomorrow	This week	This month	This year
Keep doing				
Do more of				
Do less of				

To finish off, we will ask you to set yourself **three** new SMART (specific, measurable, achievable, relevant and time-bound) goals that you will take on as a result of reading the book.

SMART Goal 1	

SMART Goal 2	

SMART Goal 3	

QUICK HELP SHEET

Congratulations on making it to the end of this workbook! By now, you will be fully prepared to start your journey as an entrepreneur. It is important to remember that there are a number of things that can't be covered within this book, and therefore it's vital to keep learning and developing yourself as a business owner.

As a reminder, you should have learned the following:

Chapter 1 Are you suitable to run a startup?

- Whether you are in the right position to start a business
- What motivates you to do what you do
- The difference between employment and self-employment

Chapter 2 Is your business idea feasible?

- How to identify what makes your business idea different
- How to evaluate the business idea
- How to determine whether the business is scalable

Chapter 3 Assembling your team and setting up the business

- Who should you bring into your team
- What questions to ask them
- Where to source free help – and when not to!

Chapter 4 Market research and understanding the business

- How to perform market research
- Types of market research
- How to evaluate the results of your research

Chapter 5 Writing a business plan

- What to include, section by section
- Do's and don'ts of preparing a business plan
- Where to take advice

Chapter 6 Raising finance

- What the options are
- How much can be raised
- How to present your case

Chapter 7 Managing your business finances

- How to effectively manage your finances within the business
- How to understand the financial reports that your accountant will give you
- How to improve the cash flow within your business

Chapter 8 Managing people

- What aspects of your business require management
- How to deal with other people that will be involved in your start up
- How to stay on the right side of the law

Chapter 9 Systemizing and scaling your business

- What the key elements of your business are
- How to structure your business to become as efficient as possible
- How to systemize your processes to allow the business to grow

Chapter 10 Promoting your business

- How to bring customers into your business
- How to monitor your marketing and advertising spend
- What to expect when marketing your business

Chapter 11 Keeping sane in business

- How to maintain an effective work–life balance
- The art of time management
- How to make sure that your business is exactly what you want

FINAL NOTE

Although this book has covered a wide range of topics, I cannot stress enough that this should only be the start of your learning about business. It's also fair to say that most of your learning will be 'on the job', during your day-to-day life as a business owner.

All that's left to say is that I wish you every success with your new startup, and please do let me know how you get on!

Twitter: www.twitter.com/CarlReader

Facebook: www.facebook.com/CarlReader

Website: www.TYCoachbook.com/Startup

BIBLIOGRAPHY

Bartkowiak, Judy, *Market Research in a Week (Teach Yourself)*, Hodder & Stoughton, 2012

Berkery, Dermot, *Raising Venture Capital for the Serious Entrepreneur*, McGraw-Hill Professional, 2007

Blick, Dee, *The 15 Essential Marketing Masterclasses for your Small Business*, Capstone, 2013

Blick, Dee, *The Ultimate Small Business Marketing Book*, Filament Publishing, 2011

Canfield, Jack, *The Success Principles*, Element, 2005

Carvill, Michelle, *The Business of Being Social*, Crimson Publishing, 2013

Clason, George S., *The Richest Man in Babylon*, Signet, 2002

Collings, Stephen, *Accounting Workbook for Dummies (UK)*, Wiley, John & Sons Incorporated; 2013

Cushway, Barry, *The Employer's Handbook 2014–15: An Essential Guide to Employment Law, Personnel Policies and Procedures*, Kogan Page 2014

Duckett, Brian, *How to Franchise your Business*, How To Books, 2011

Duncan, Lee, *How to Double your Business*, Financial Times/Prentice Hall, 2012

Evans, Vaughan, *The FT Guide to Writing a Business Plan: How to Win Backing to Start Up or Grow Your Business*, Financial Times/Prentice Hall, 2011

Godin, Seth, *Poke the Box*, The Domino Project, 2011

Hague, Paul et al, *Market Research in Practice: A Guide to the Basics*, Kogan Page, 2004

Kriel, Nicky, *How to Twitter for Business Success*, The Other Publishing Company, 2013

Mason, Roger, *Bookkeeping and Accounting in a Week (Teach Yourself)*, Hodder & Stoughton 2012

Paul, Debra et al., *Business Analysis*, BCS 2010

Priestley, Daniel, *Entrepreneur Revolution*, Capstone, 2013

Robbins, Antony, *Awaken the Giant Within*, Pocket books, 2001

Rosenberg, Merrick et al, *Taking Flight! Master the DISC Styles to Transform Your Career, Your Relationships . . . Your Life*, FT Press, 2012

Sawyer, Clive, *How to Franchise Your Business: The Plain Speaking Guide*, Live It, 2011

Thomas, Bryony, *Watertight Marketing*, Ecademy Press Limited, 2013

Thompson, Jody, *Why Managing Sucks and How to Fix It: A Results-Only Guide to Taking Control of Work, Not People,* John Wiley & Sons, 2013

Thompson, Jody, *Why Work Sucks and How to Fix It: The Results-Only Revolution,* Portfolio, 2011

Tiffany, Paul et al, *Business Plans for Dummies,* HarperAudio, 2007

Tracy, Brian, *Goals! How to Get Everything You Want, Faster Than You Ever Thought Possible,* Berret-Koehler Publishers 2010

USEFUL RESOURCES

How to choose an accountant:

http://www.startupdonut.co.uk/startup/tax-and-national-insurance/
accounting-and-bookkeeping/q-a-choosing-an-accountant

How to choose a solicitor:

http://www.lawsociety.org.uk/for-the-public/using-a-solicitor/

How to choose a consultant or coach:

http://www.passionforbusiness.com/articles/select-small-business-coach.htm

Companies House:

http://www.companieshouse.gov.uk

.gov.uk video on Market Research:

https://www.gov.uk/market-research-business

The Market Research Society:

https://www.mrs.org.uk/

Consolidated list of business plan information:

http://www.greatbusiness.gov.uk/the-how-to-write-a-business-plan-guide/

Online business plan templates:

www.bplans.co.uk

General guides to startup funding

http://startups.co.uk/raising-finance/

http://www.smallbusiness.co.uk/starting-a-business/start-up-funding/

Venture Capital guide

http://www.bothsidesofthetable.com/

INDEX

INDEX

A

ACAS code of practice 155
accountants 47, 56, 99
accounting software 133
accruals 127
action plans 82, 97, 224–5
advertising 196
AIDA (Attention Interest Desire Action) 187
Amazon 20–1
Amstrad E-mailer 24
angel investment 107, 108–9
Annual Accounting Scheme 132
Annual Holiday Entitlement 153–4
appraising job candidates 150
Atari Jaguar 24
attainable goals 13

B

balance sheets 125–6
bank account monitoring 128
bank loans/managers 47, 56, 99, 105, 110, 114, 129
bookkeeping 119
bookkeeping courses 122
books, and business skills 214
brand development 183–5
brand logo 183
brand protection 186–7
business advisors 28, 56, 100
business aims 42
business briefing 93
business coaches 57
business colleagues 100
business consultants 56–7
business formats 59–62
business growth 175–9
business performance appraisal 162
business plans 88–101
business processes 53, 161–2
business promotion 182–99
business support 220–1
business system consolidation 173
business team members 46–57
business viability 28

C

Cash Accounting Scheme 131
cash flow management 127–9
cash flow, and profit 119
cash flow projections 96
cashflow quadrant 10
checklist system 166
college courses, and business skills 211
Community Interest Companies 62
Companies House 62
competitor analysis 28–30
competitor research 67, 81
corporation tax 130
creators 53
credit control 128
CRM (customer relationship management) 169–70
crowd funding 108
current assets 125
current liabilities 125
customer referrals 196
cut-off adjustments 127
CVs, in business plans 95

D

data availablity 77
data requirements 73–7
debtors 128
desk research 68
desktop software 119
direct mail shots 195
DISC profiling 146
disciplinary processes 155–6
discrimination 154–5
domain names 183
due dates 128

E

E-Myth 11
eBay 20–1
elevator pitch 20, 25–7
email marketing 188
employment law 153–6

235